This
Book Belongs
To:

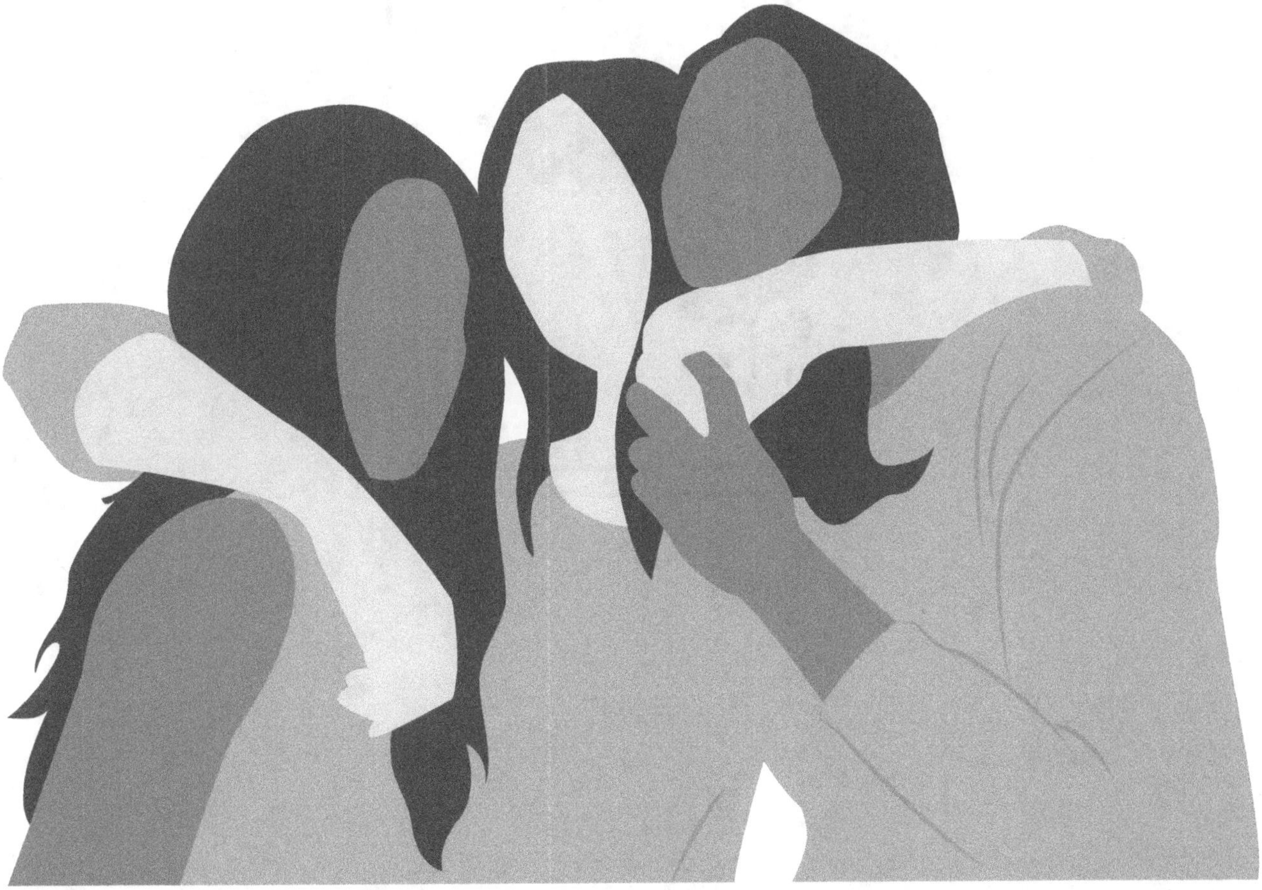

_____

_____

Copyrighted© By: April King 2022

Dear Customer,
I hope you enjoy my Extraordinary Women Coloring Book.

I also hope you find these motivational quotes uplifting as you unwind, relax, and find some time for yourself to enjoy the little things in life like....
Coloring 🏷️

P.S. If you have a moment can you please leave a review on this book by searching April King Coloring Books (or Book Name) on Amazon. I would Truly Appreciate it.

Copyrighted©   By: April King 2022

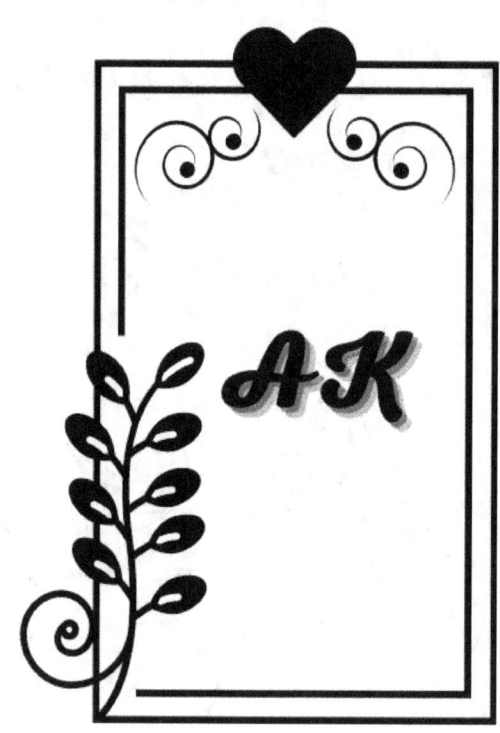

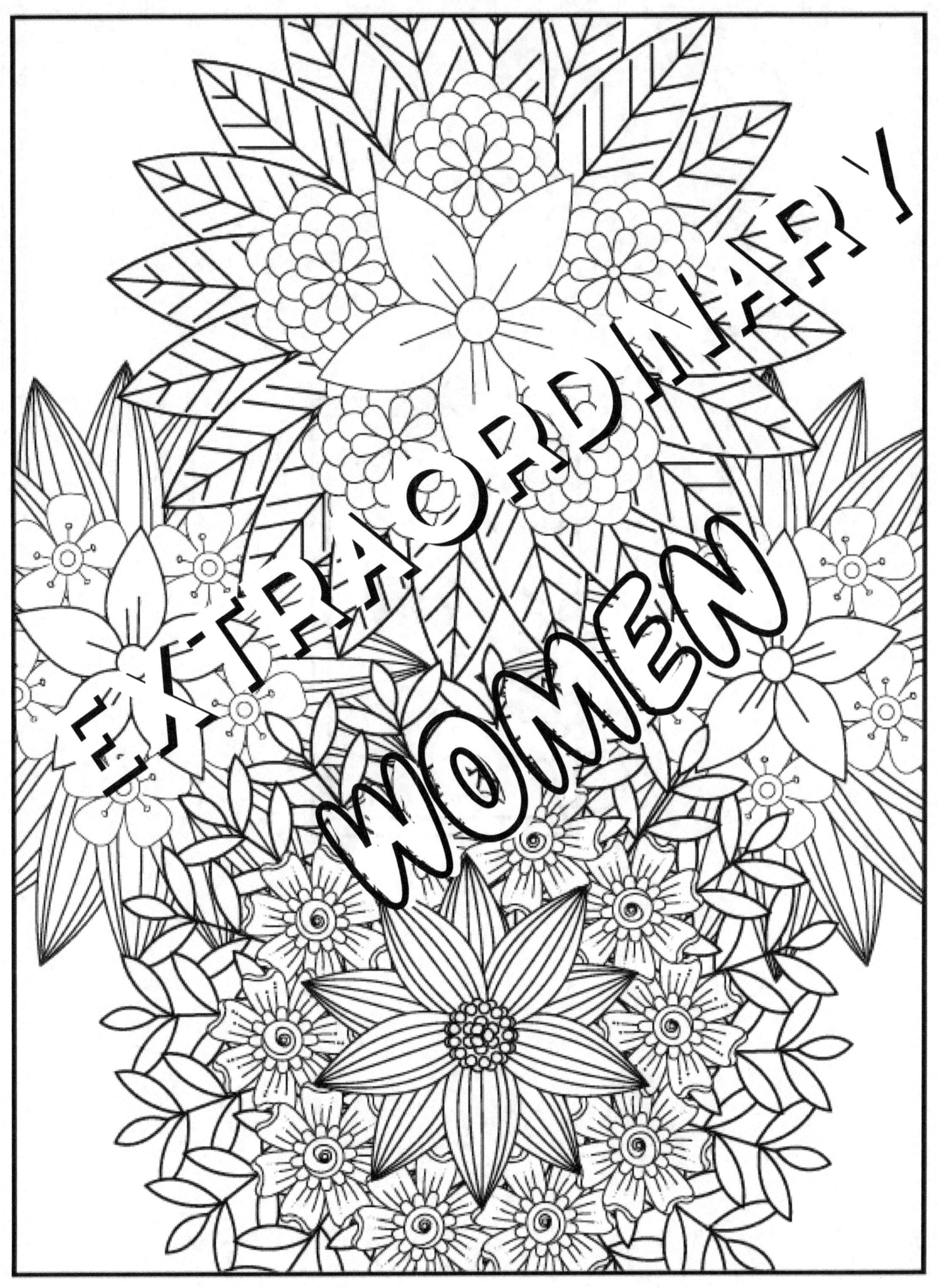

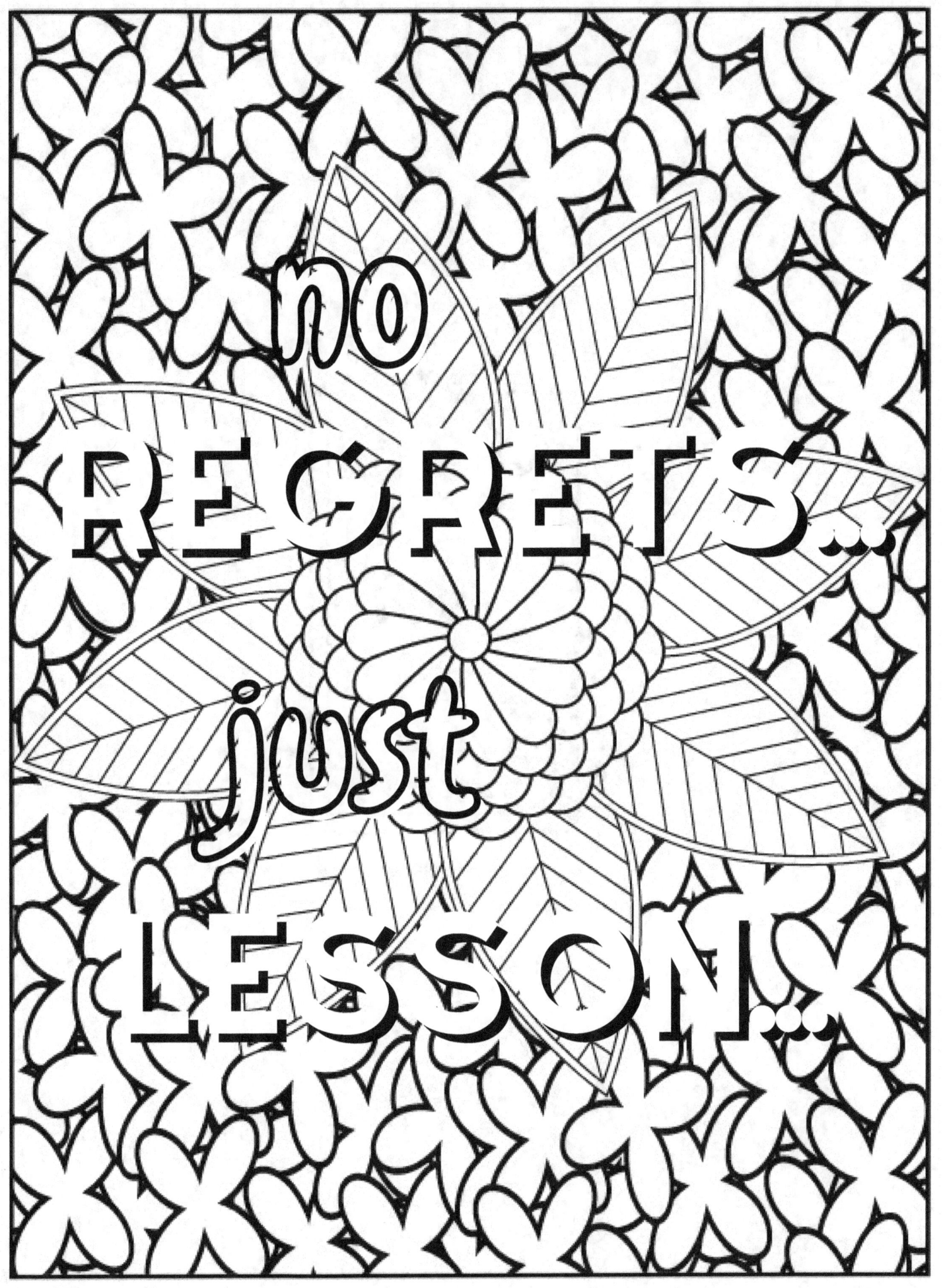

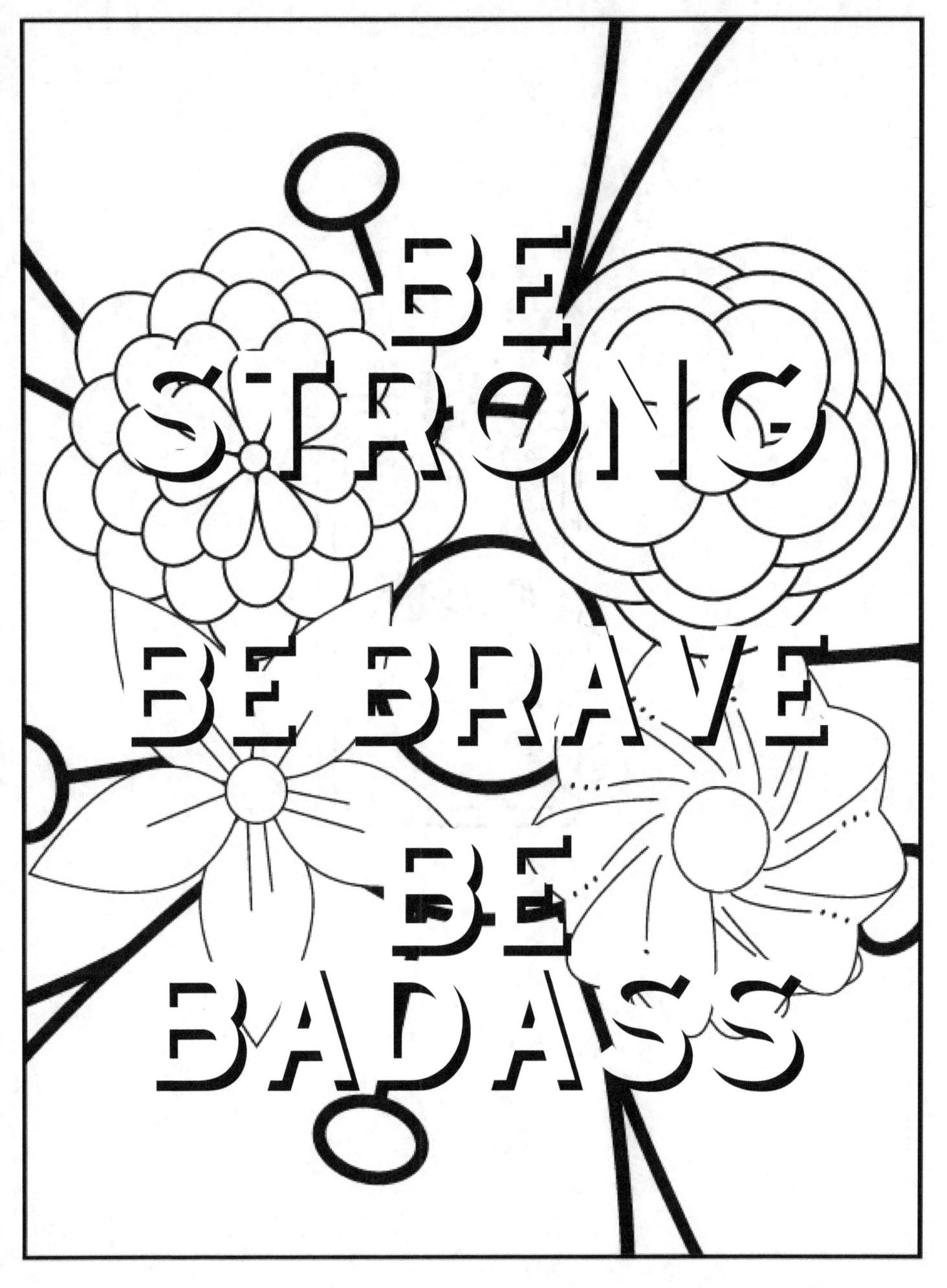

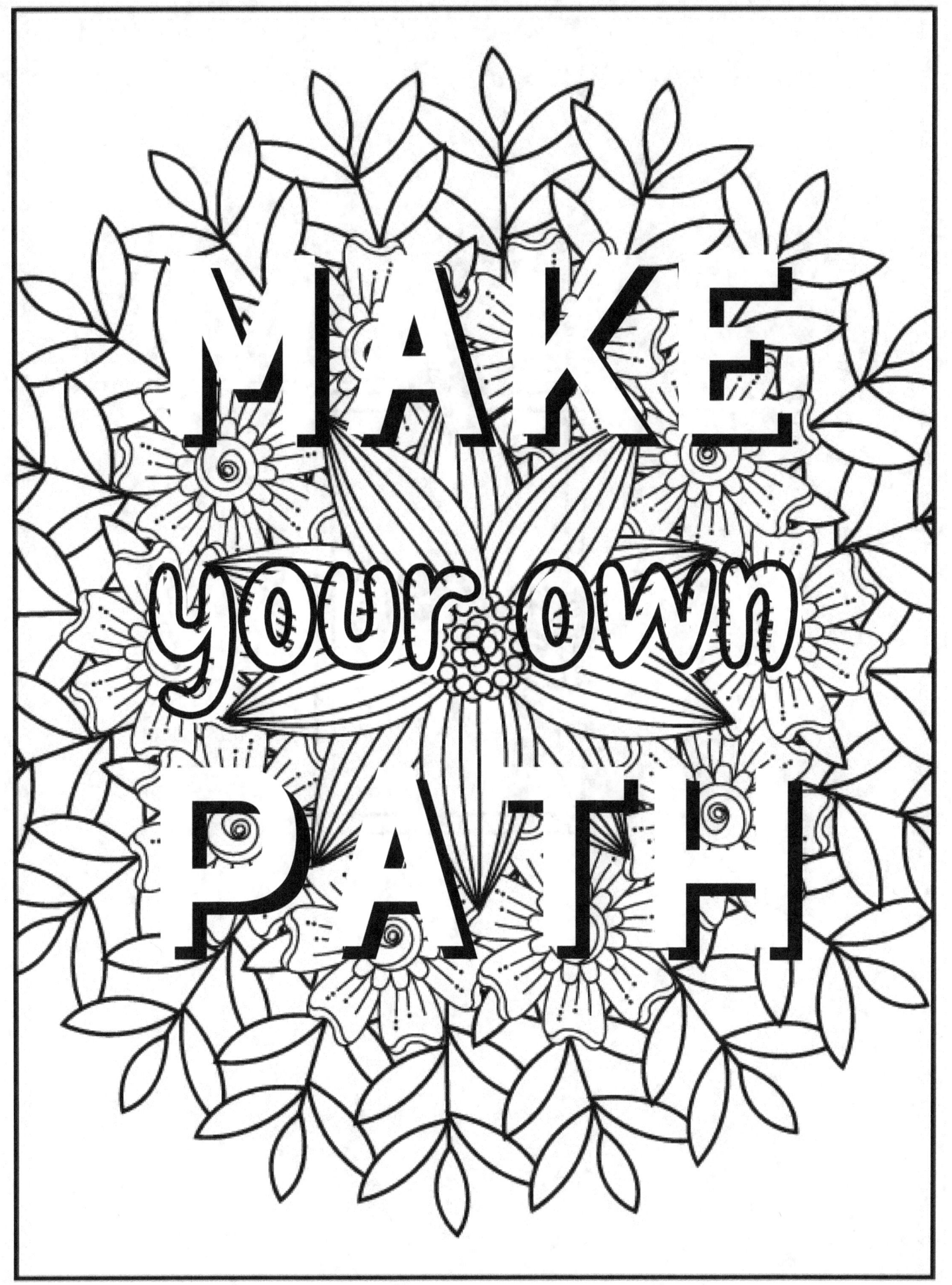

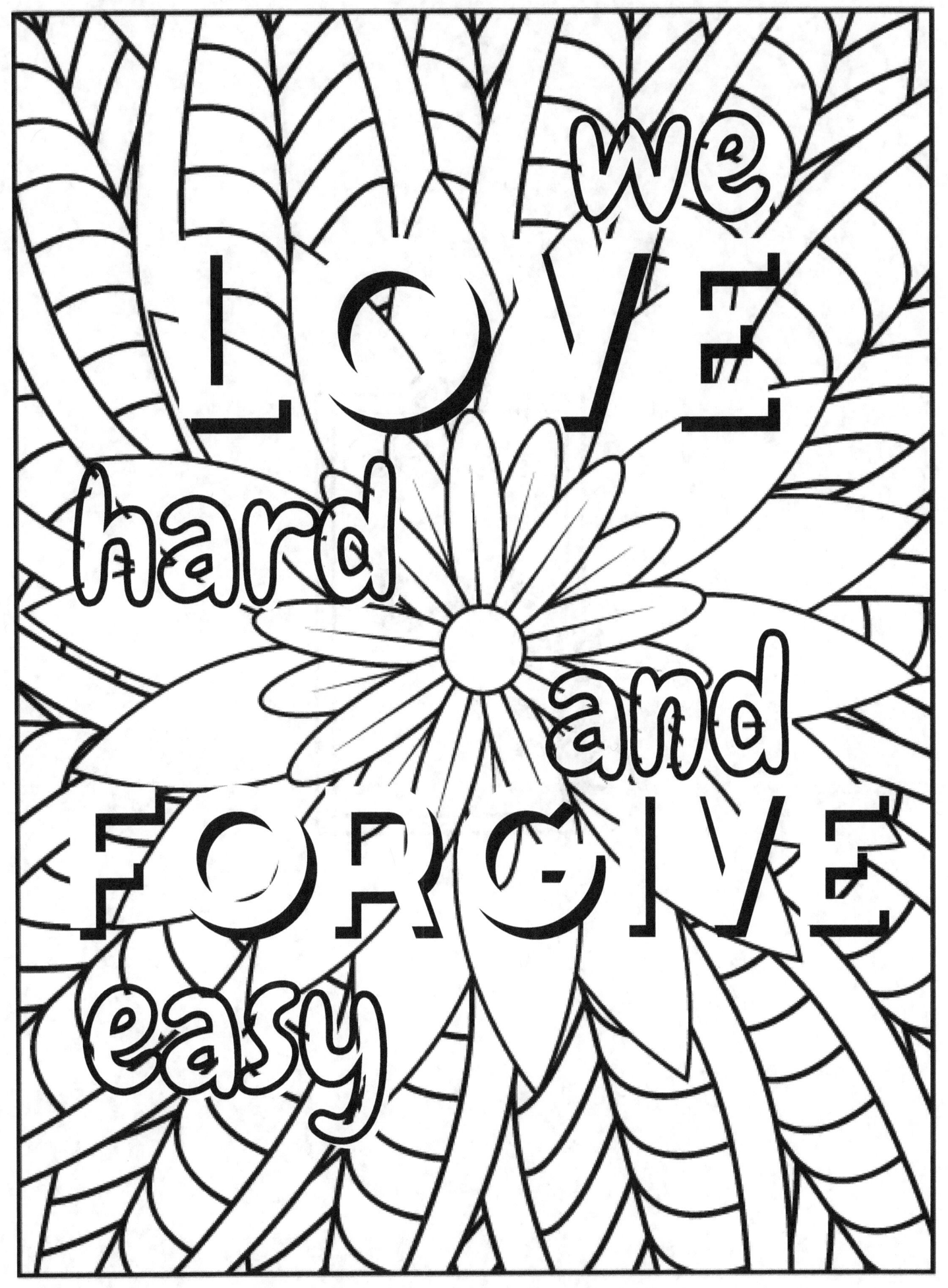

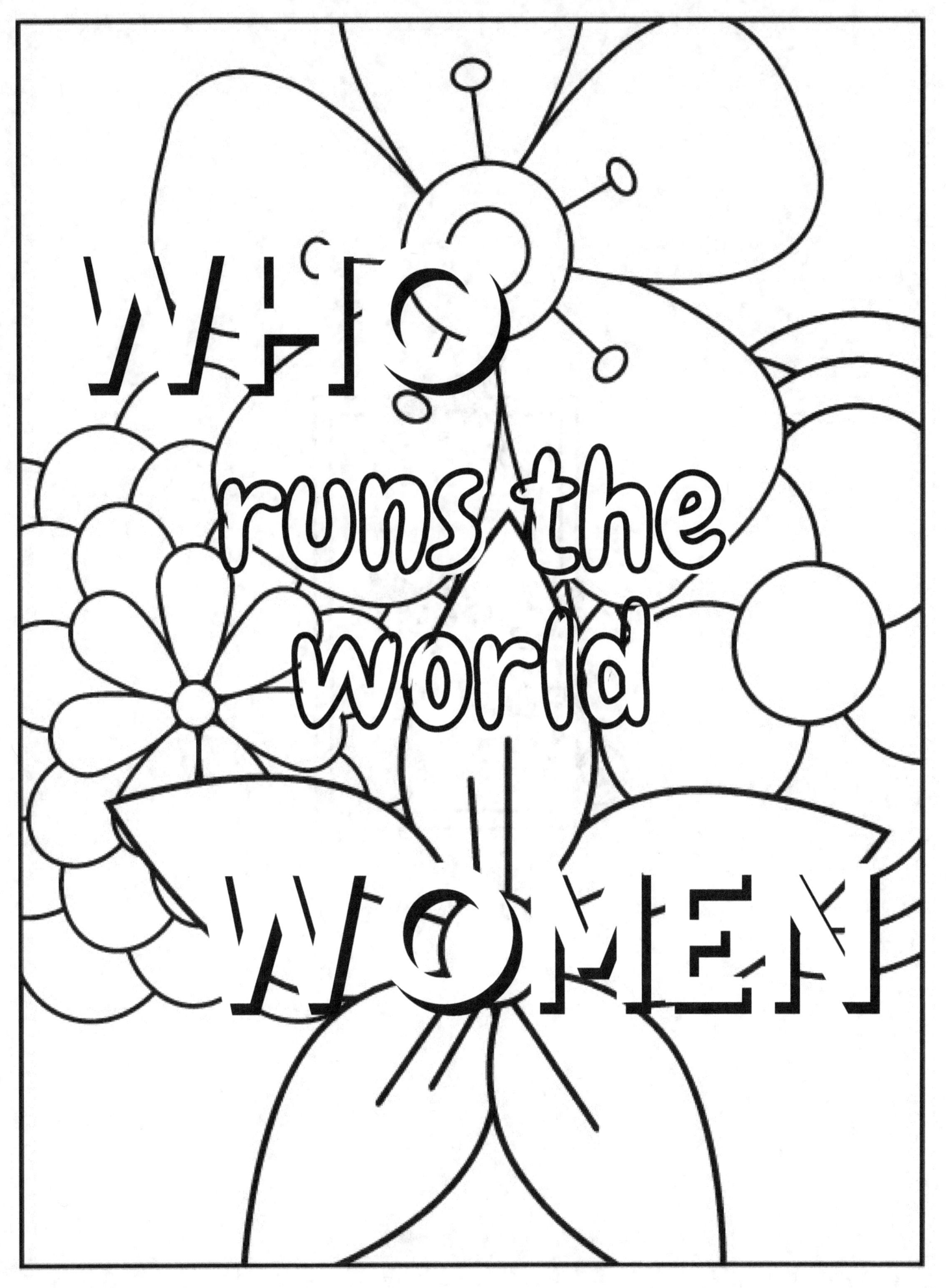

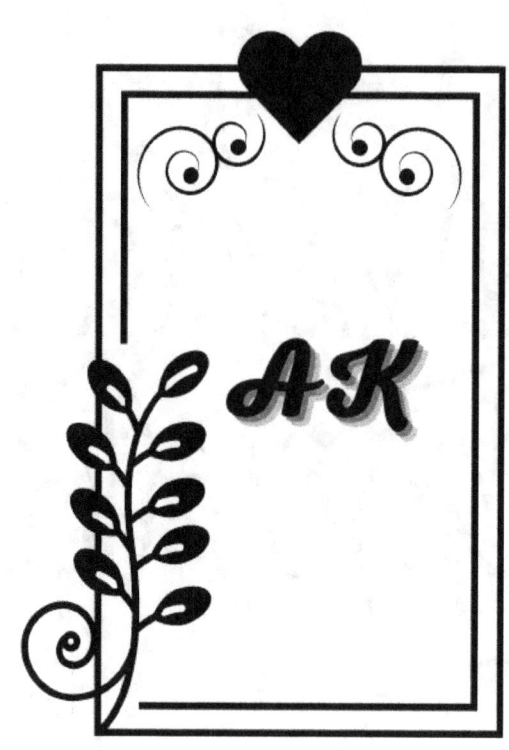

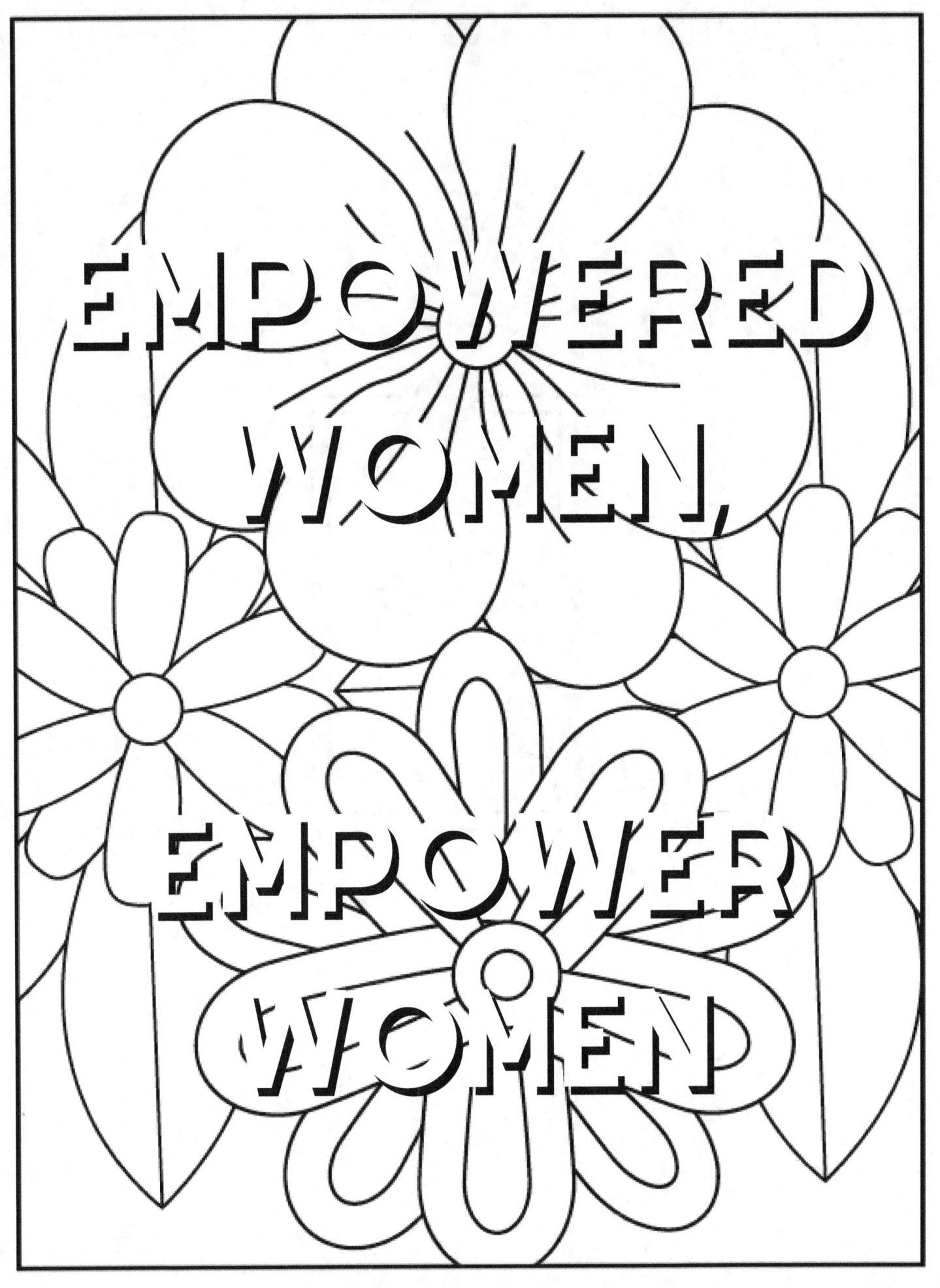

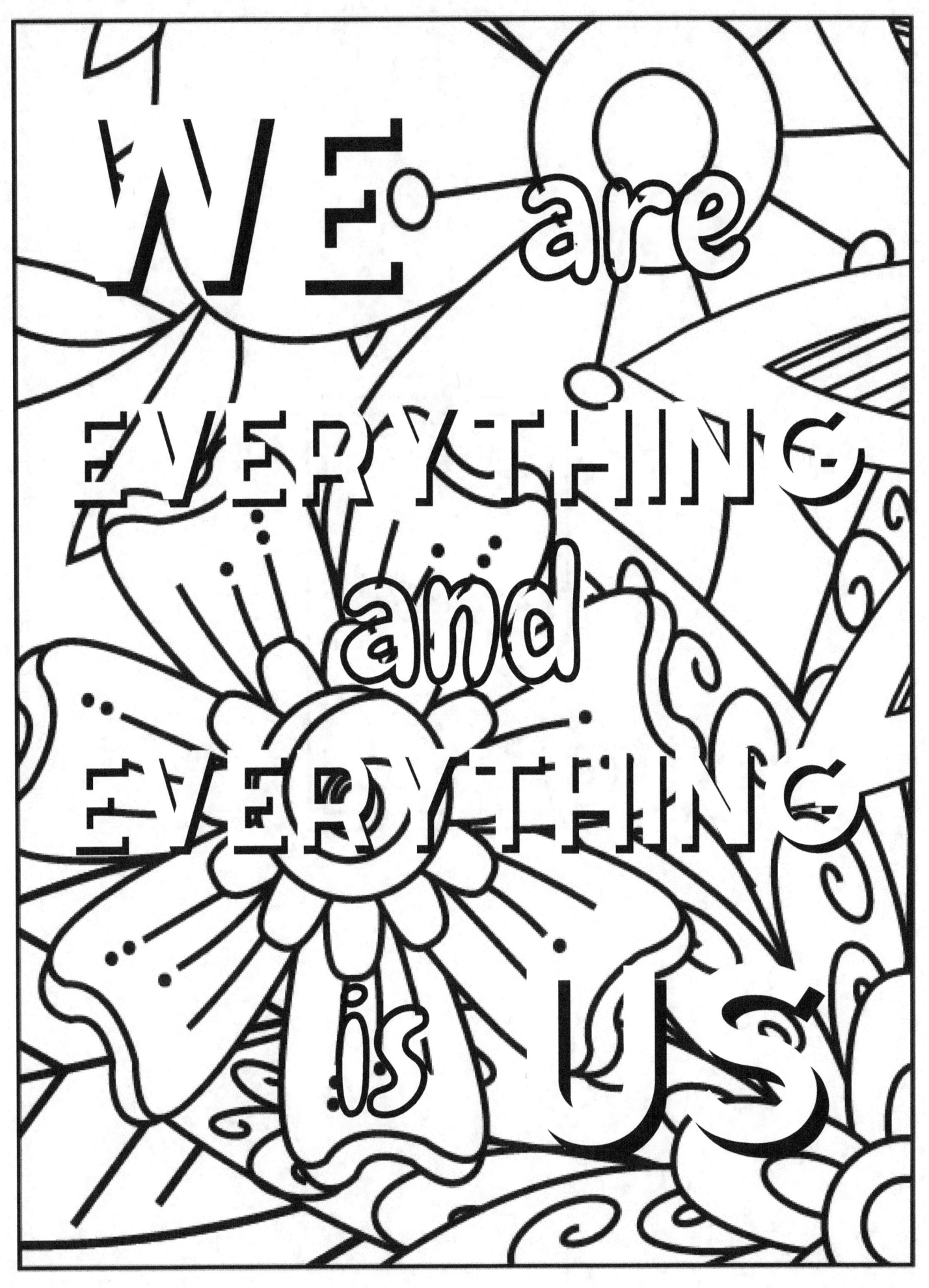

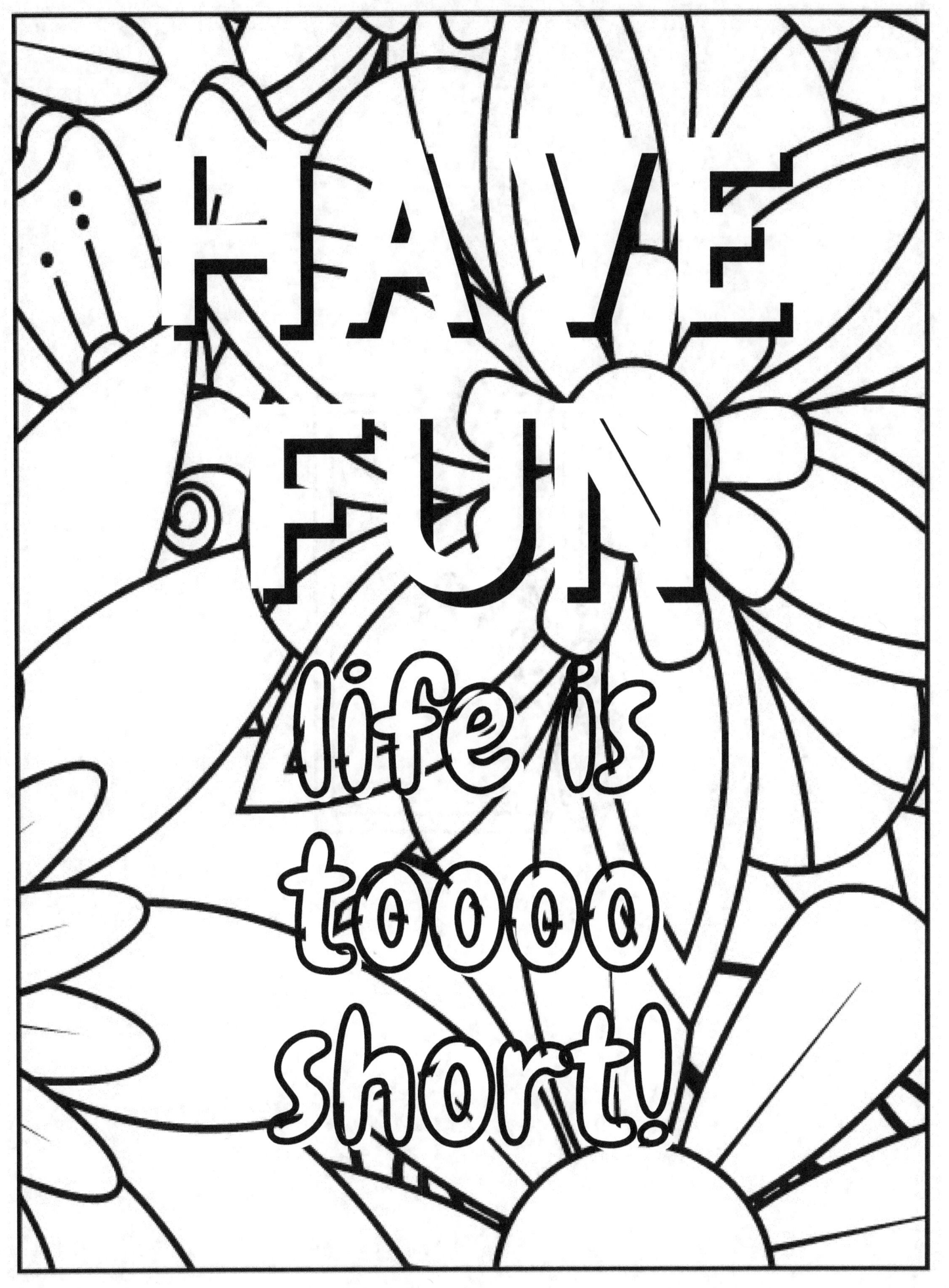

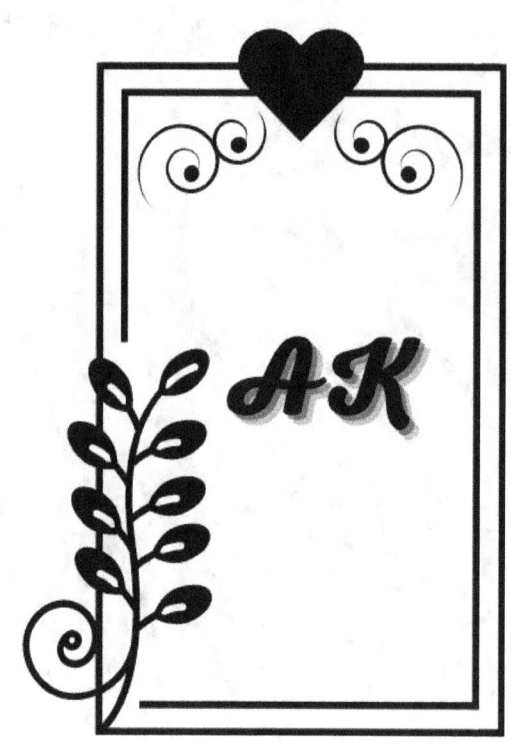

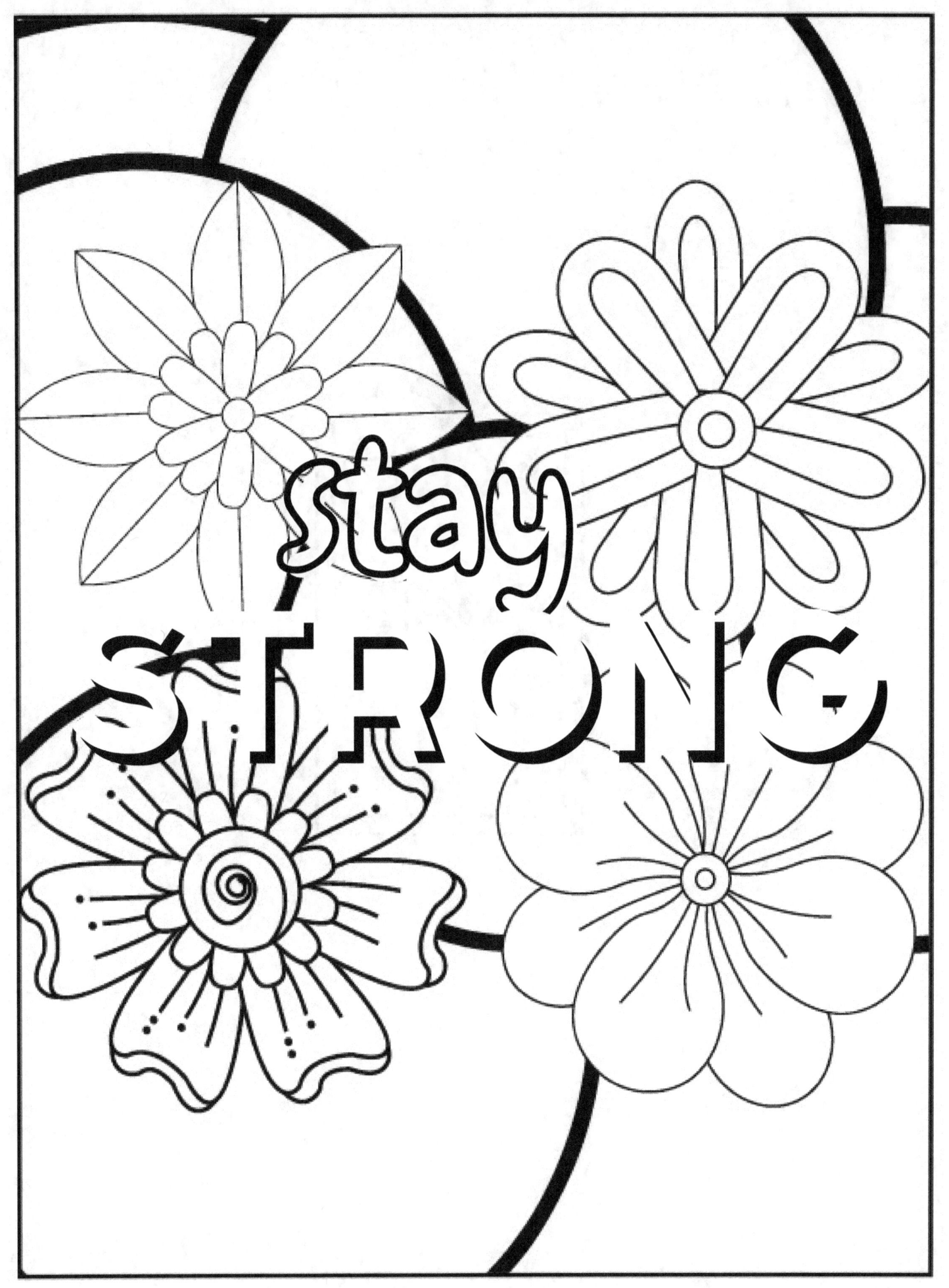

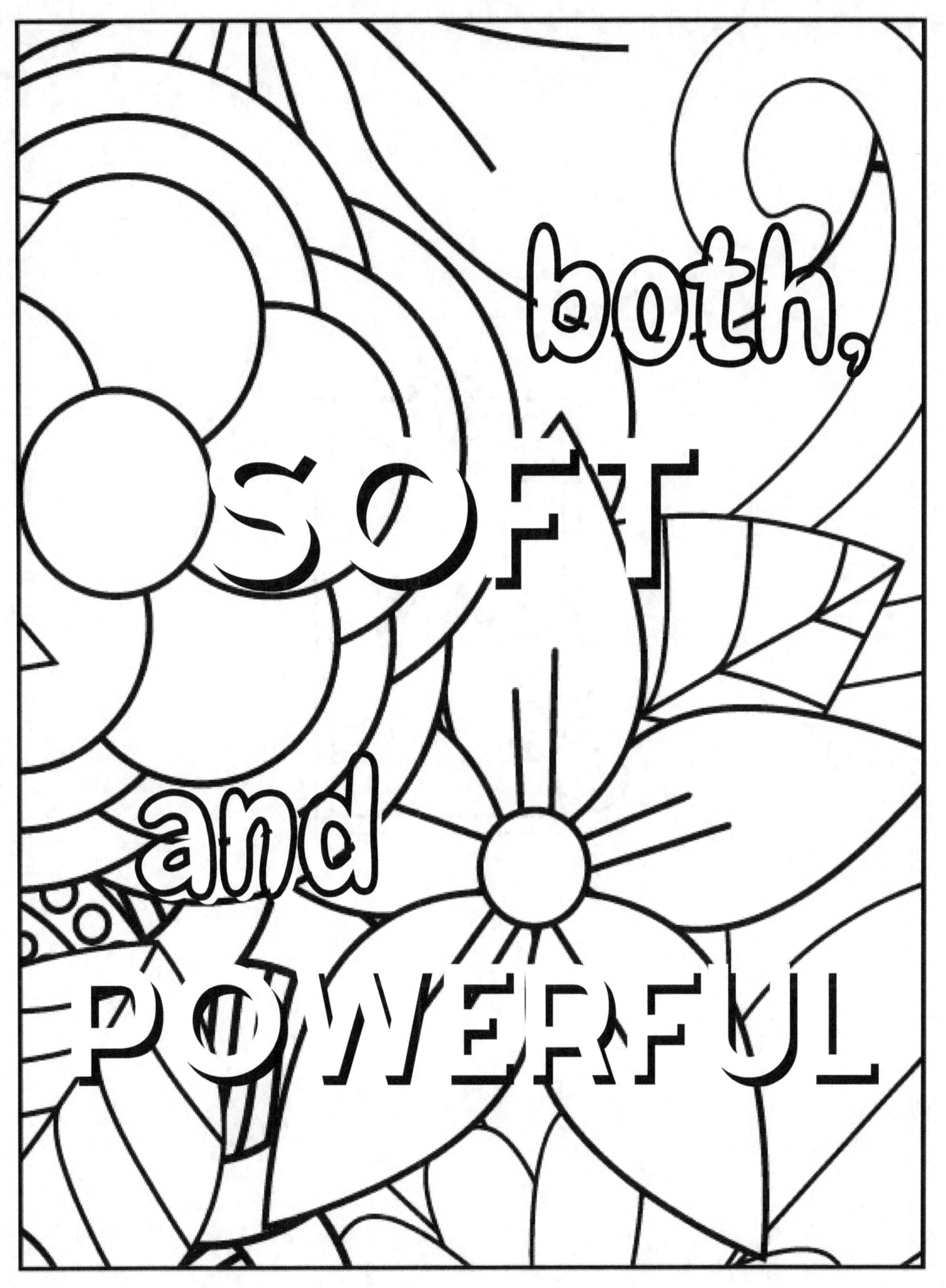

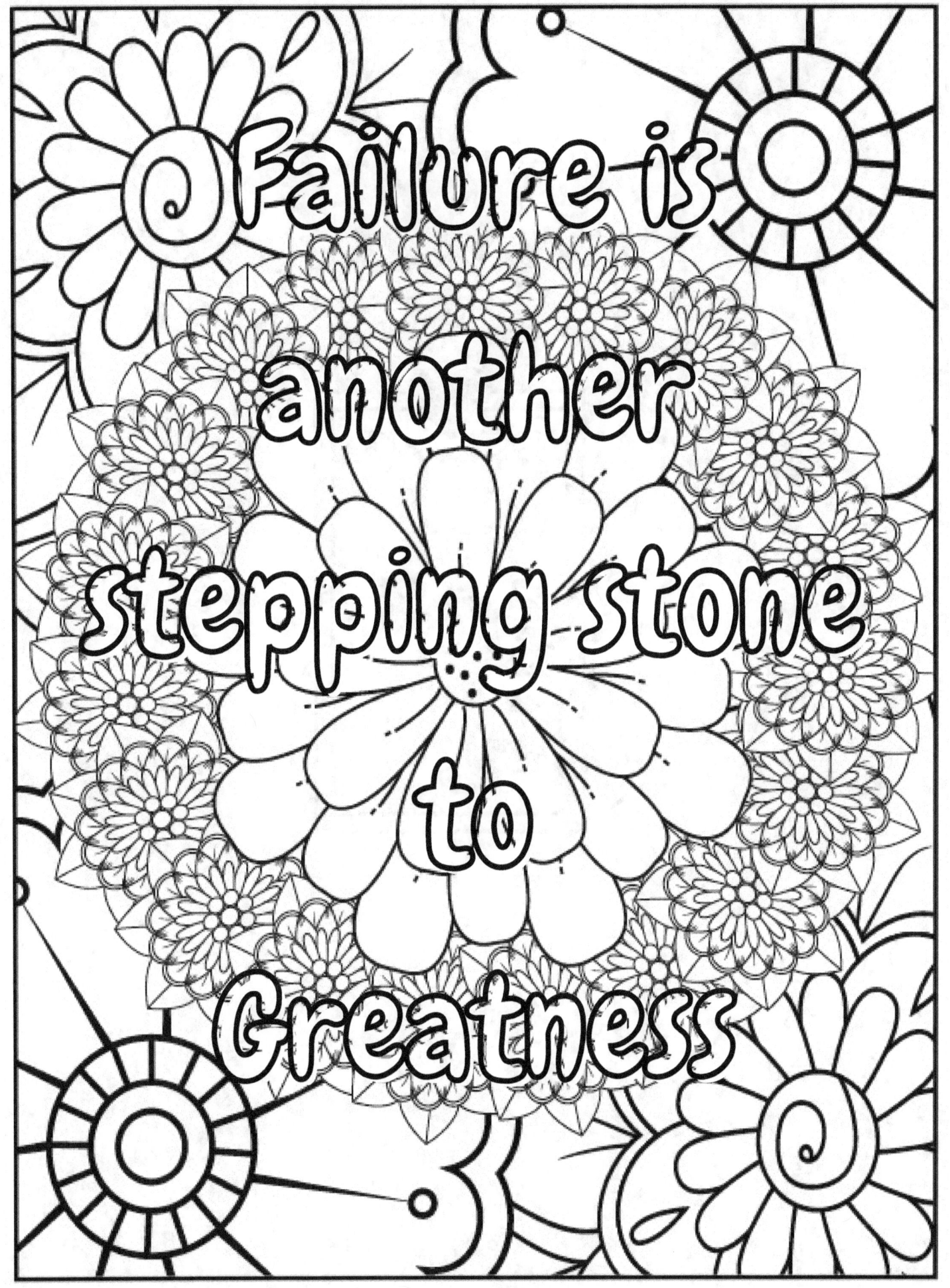

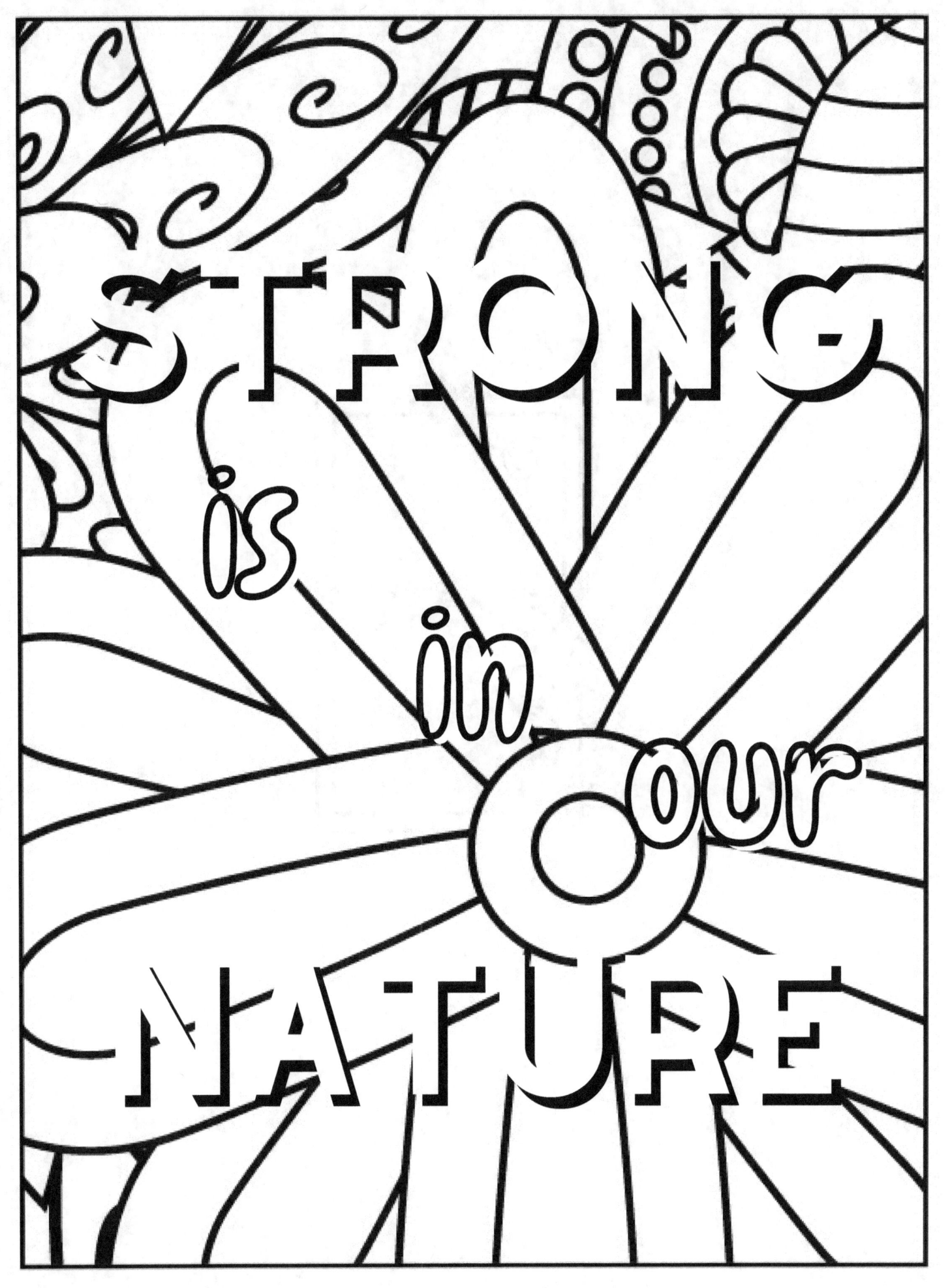

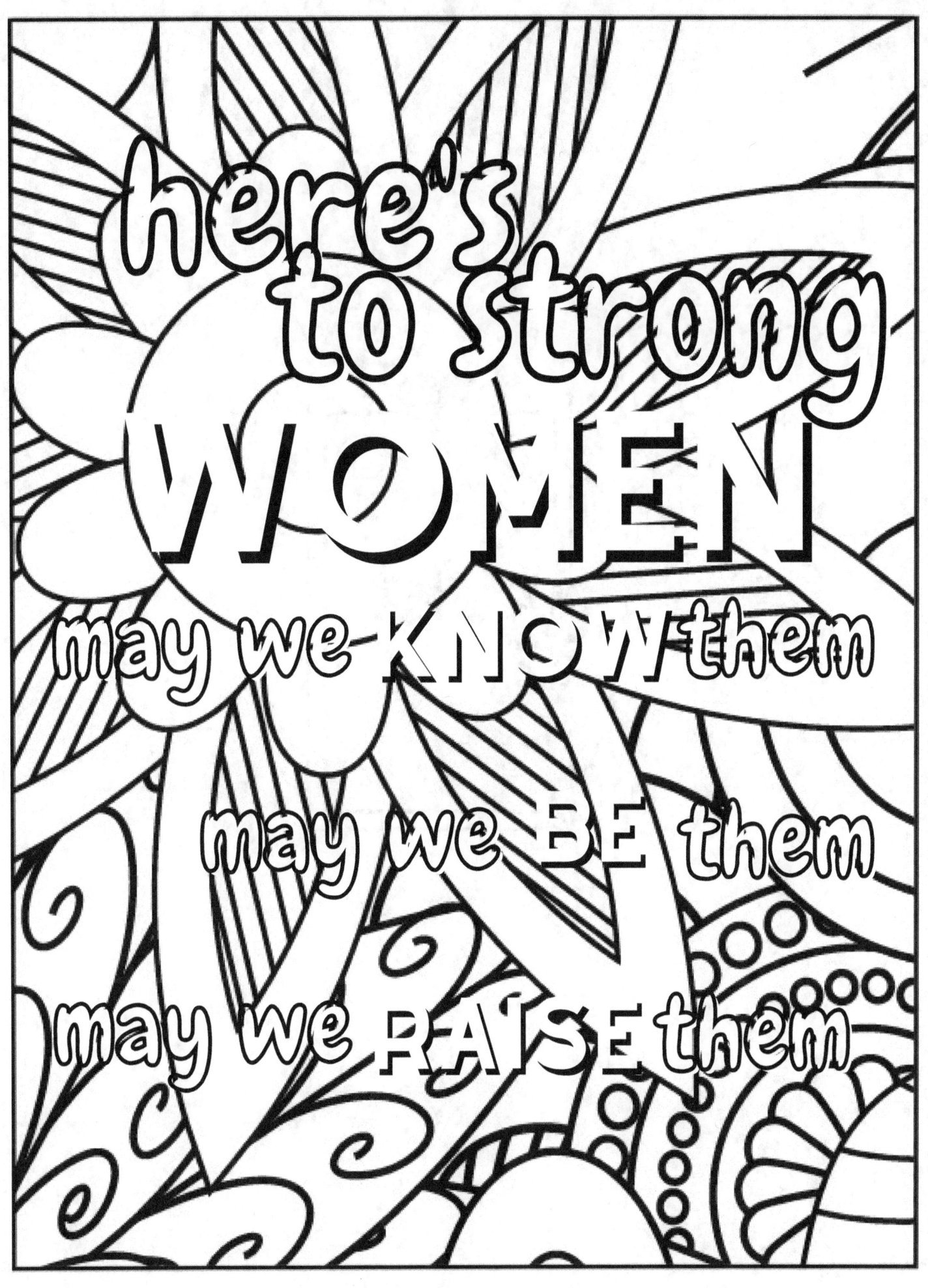

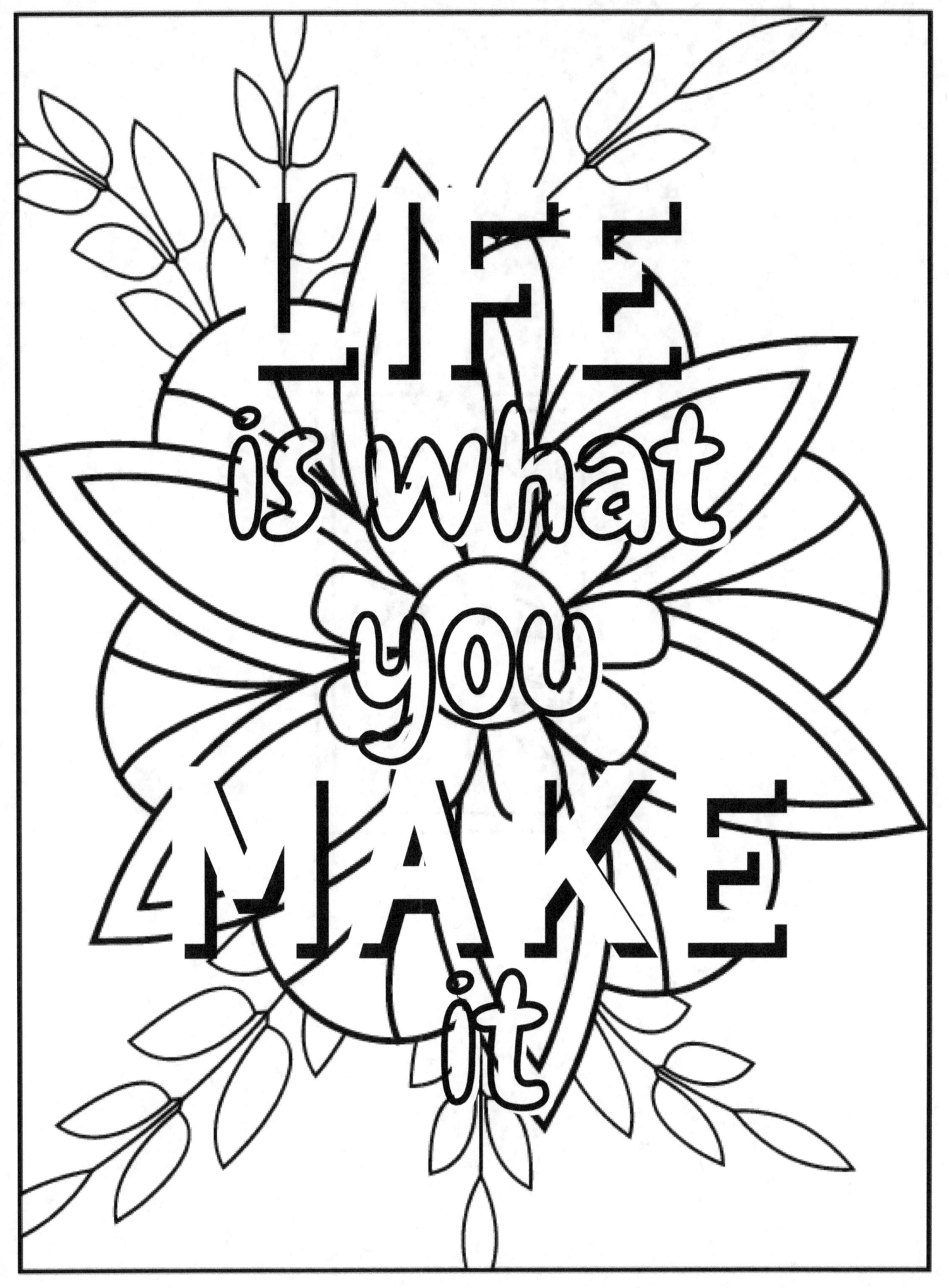

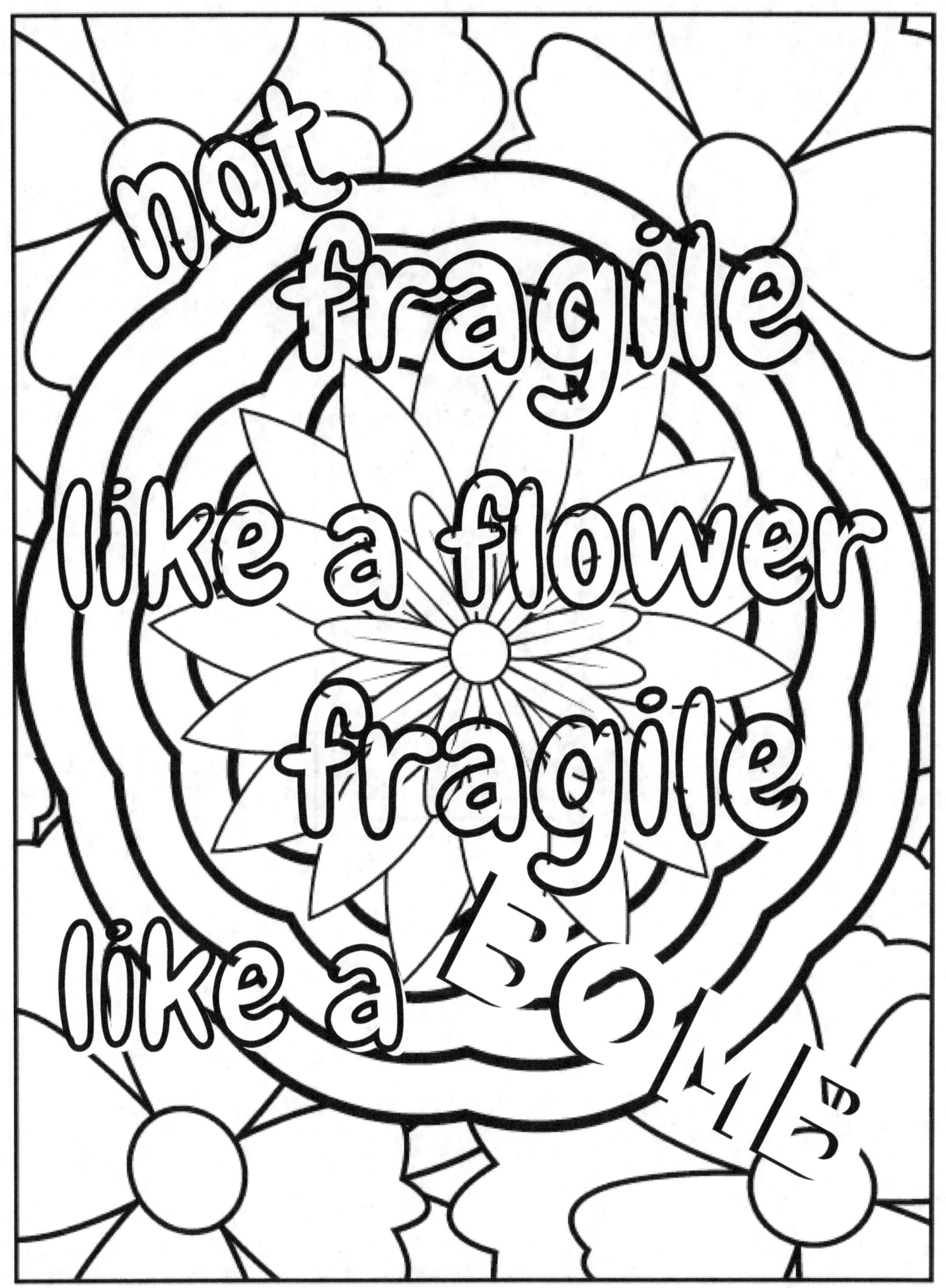

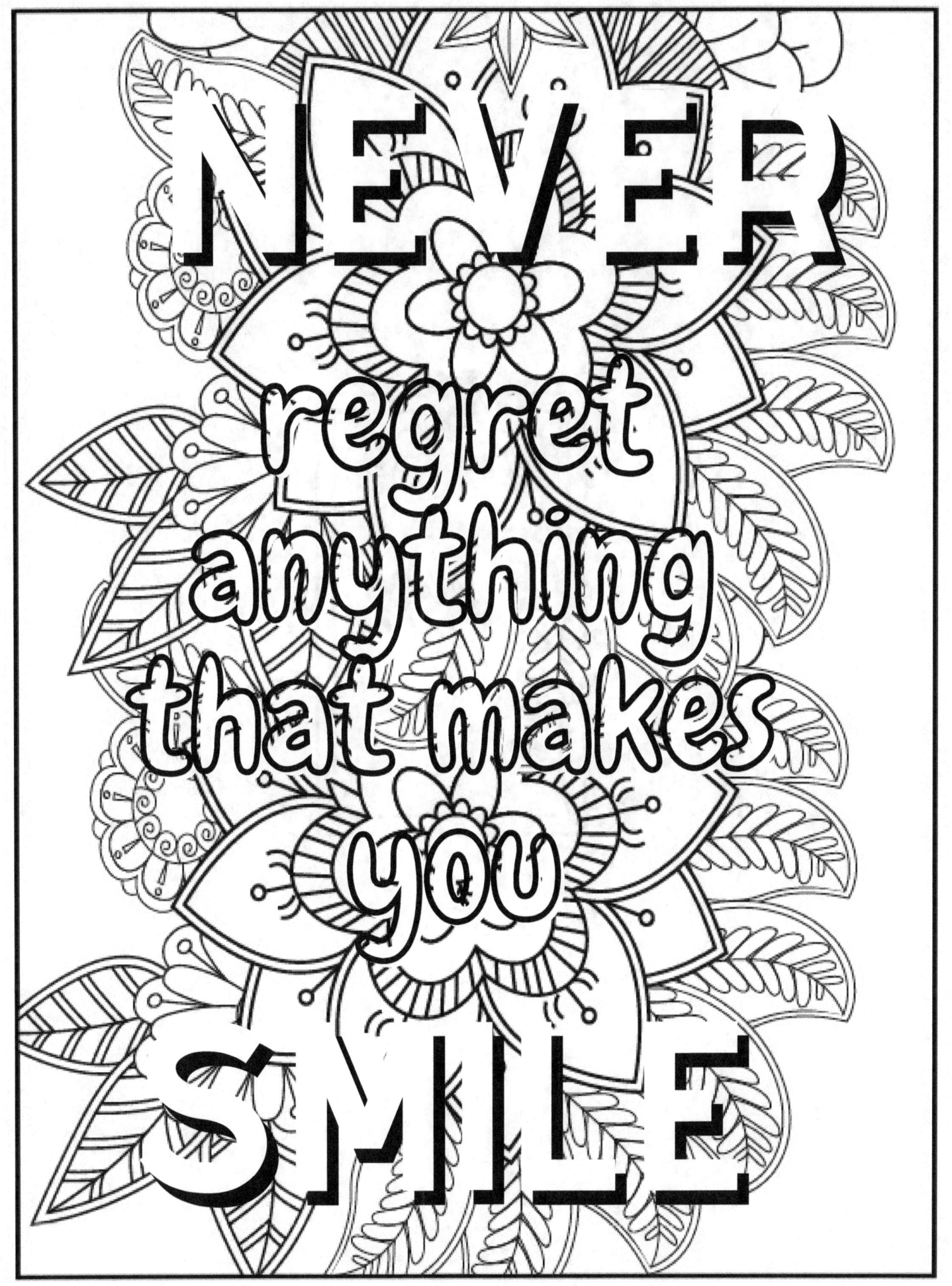

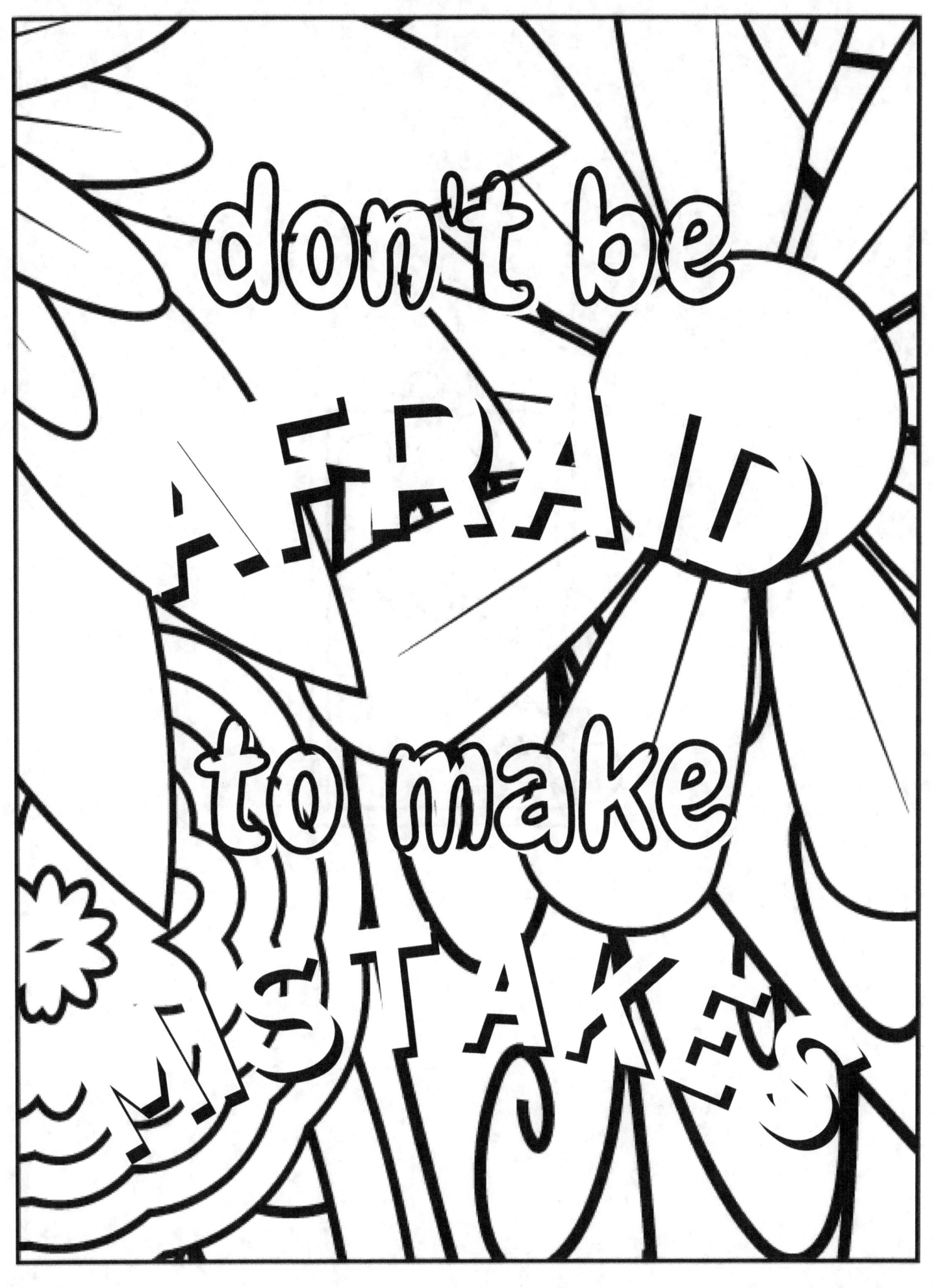

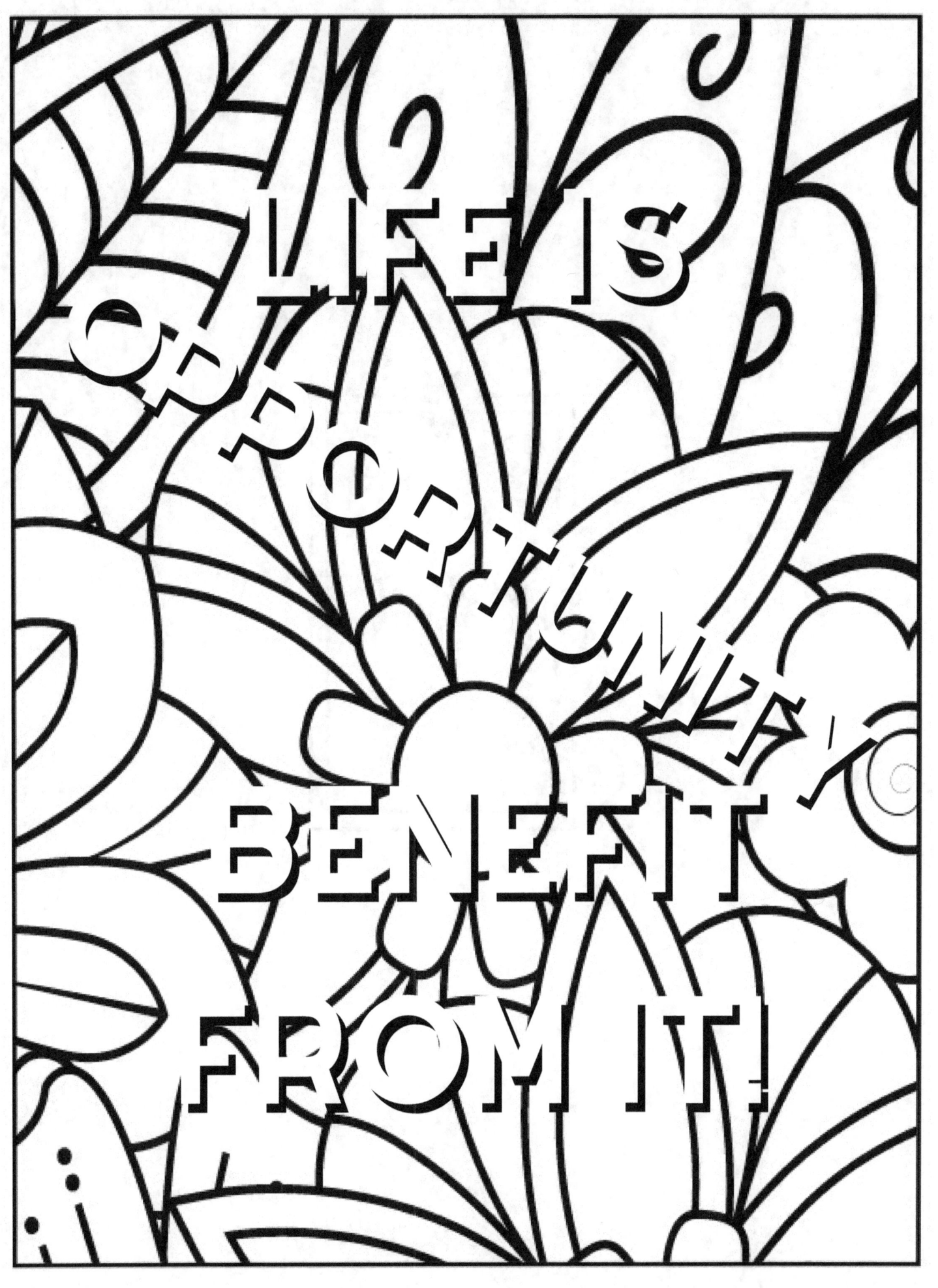

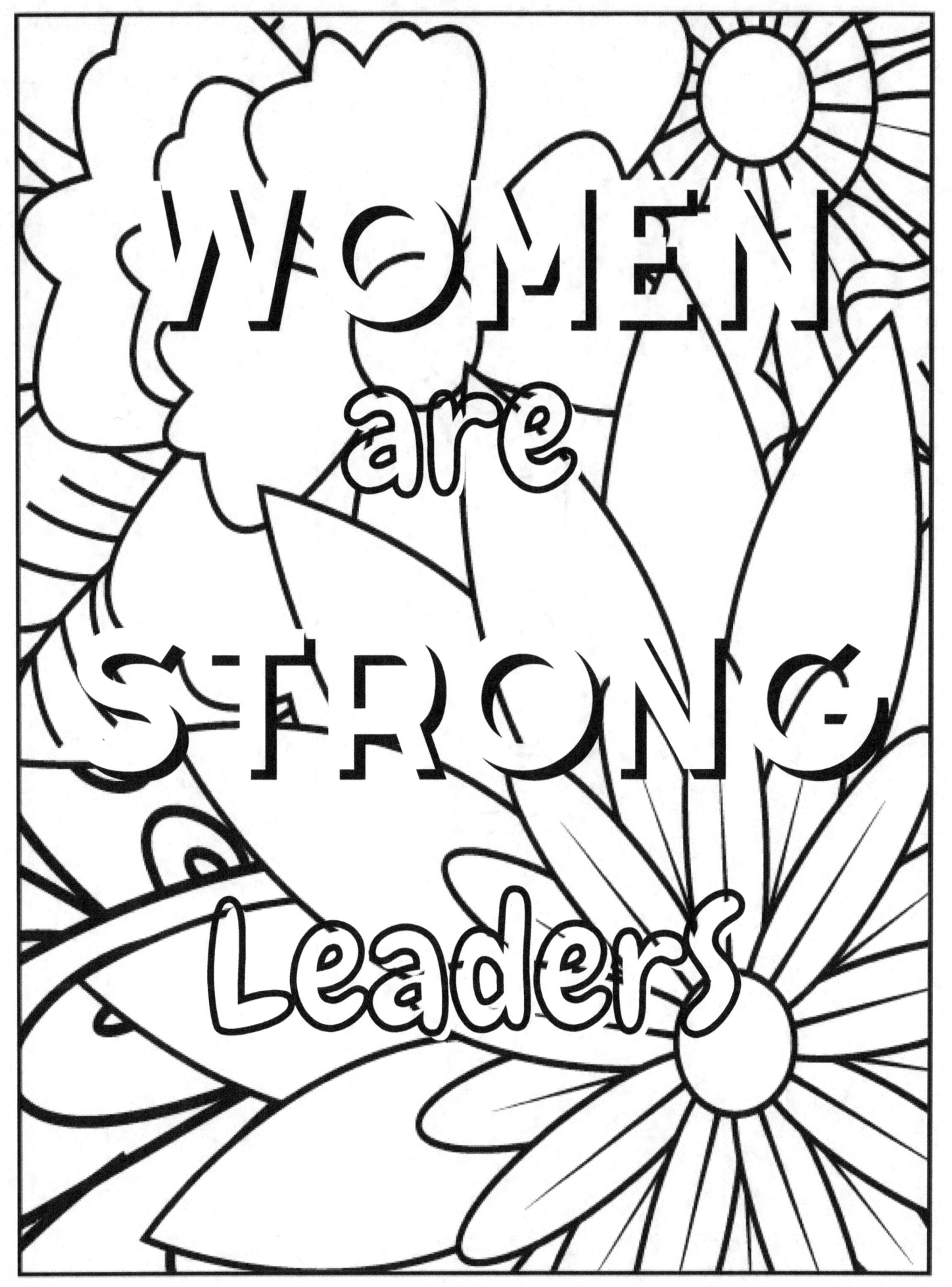

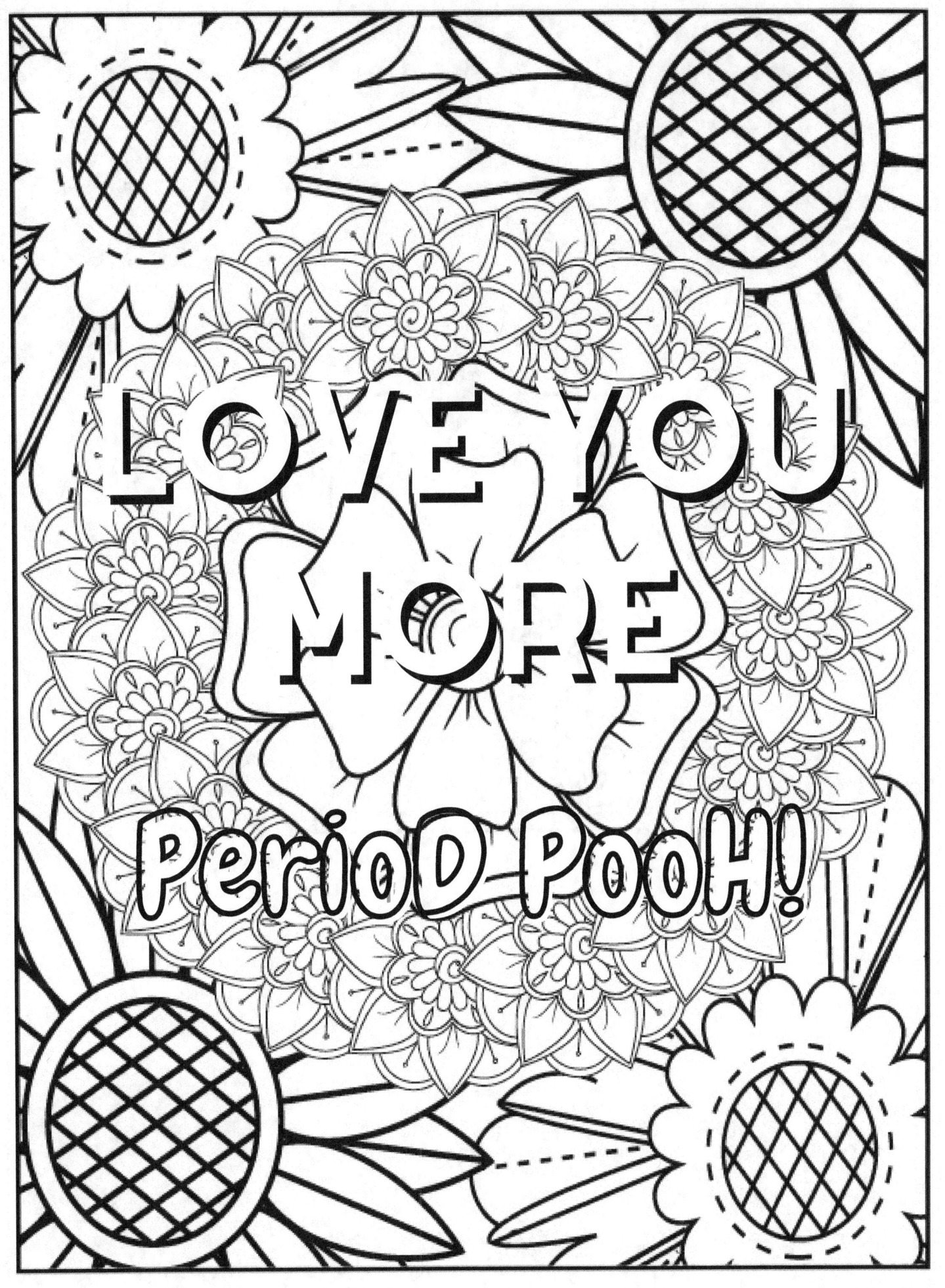

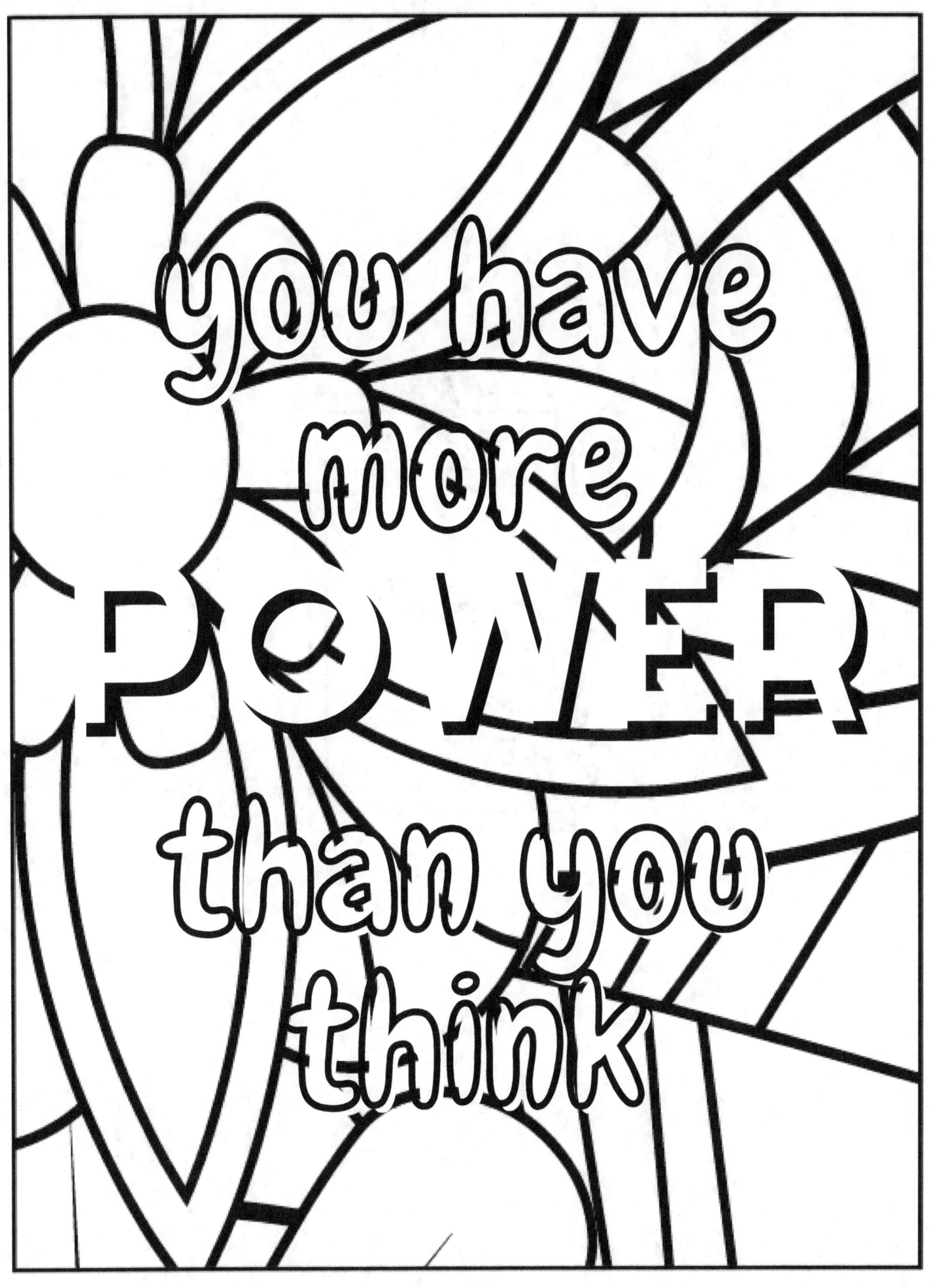

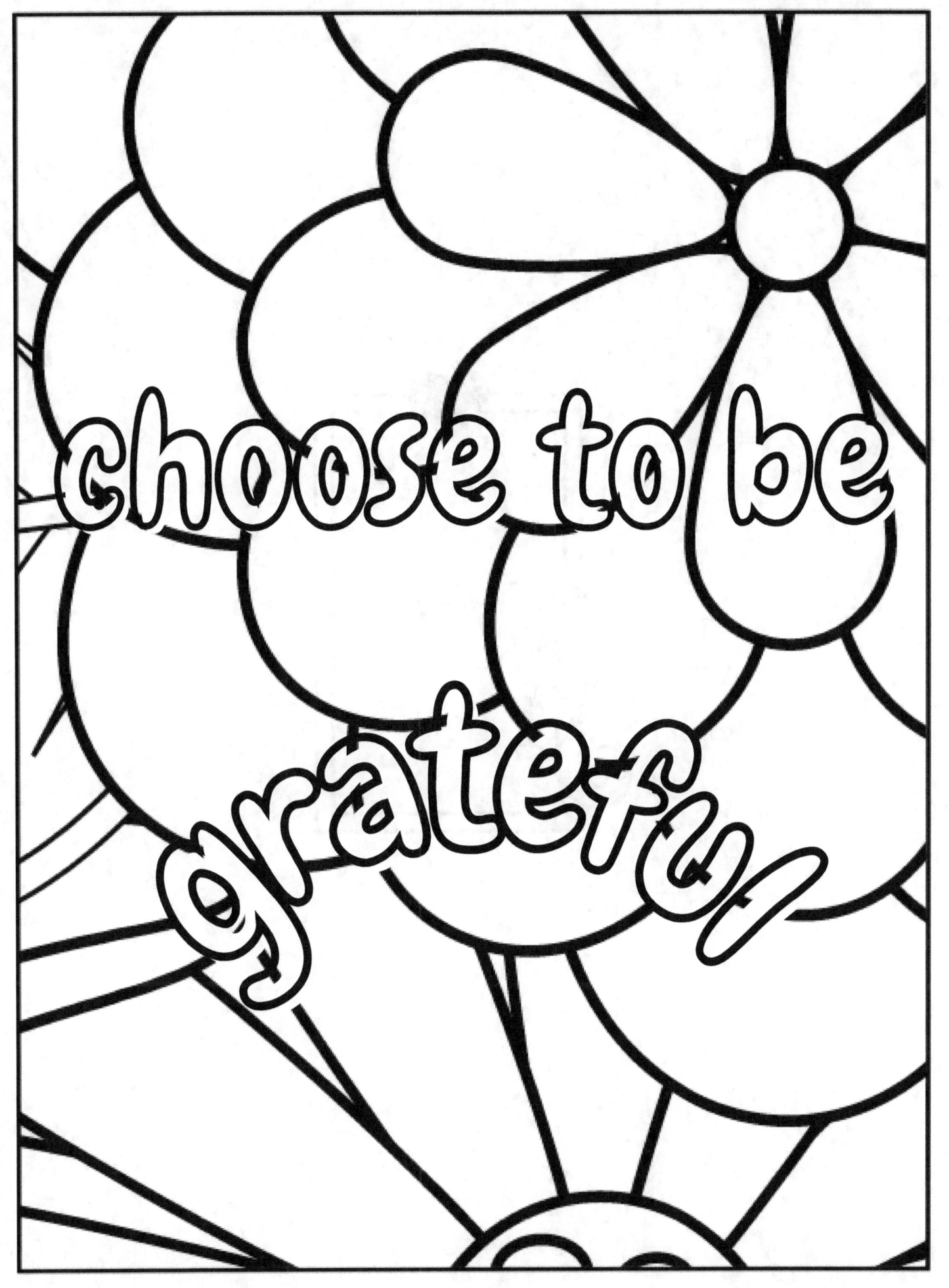

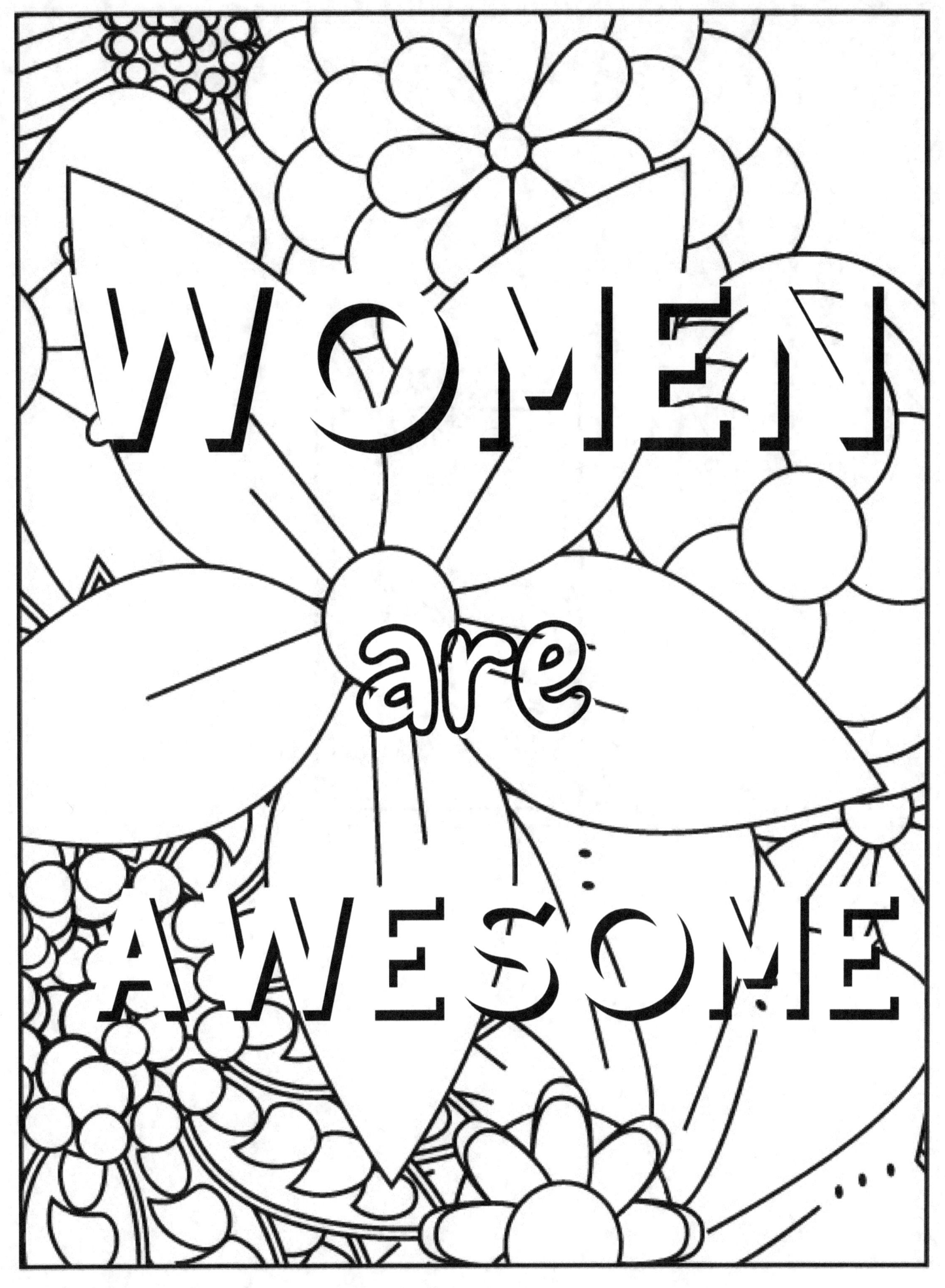

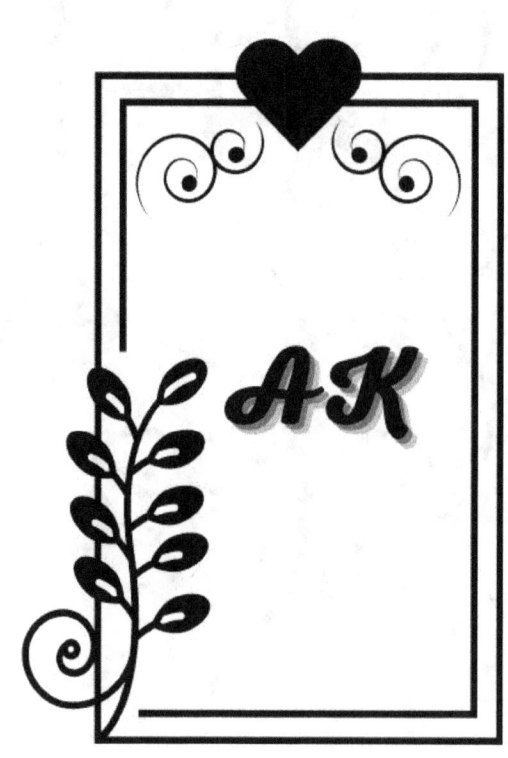

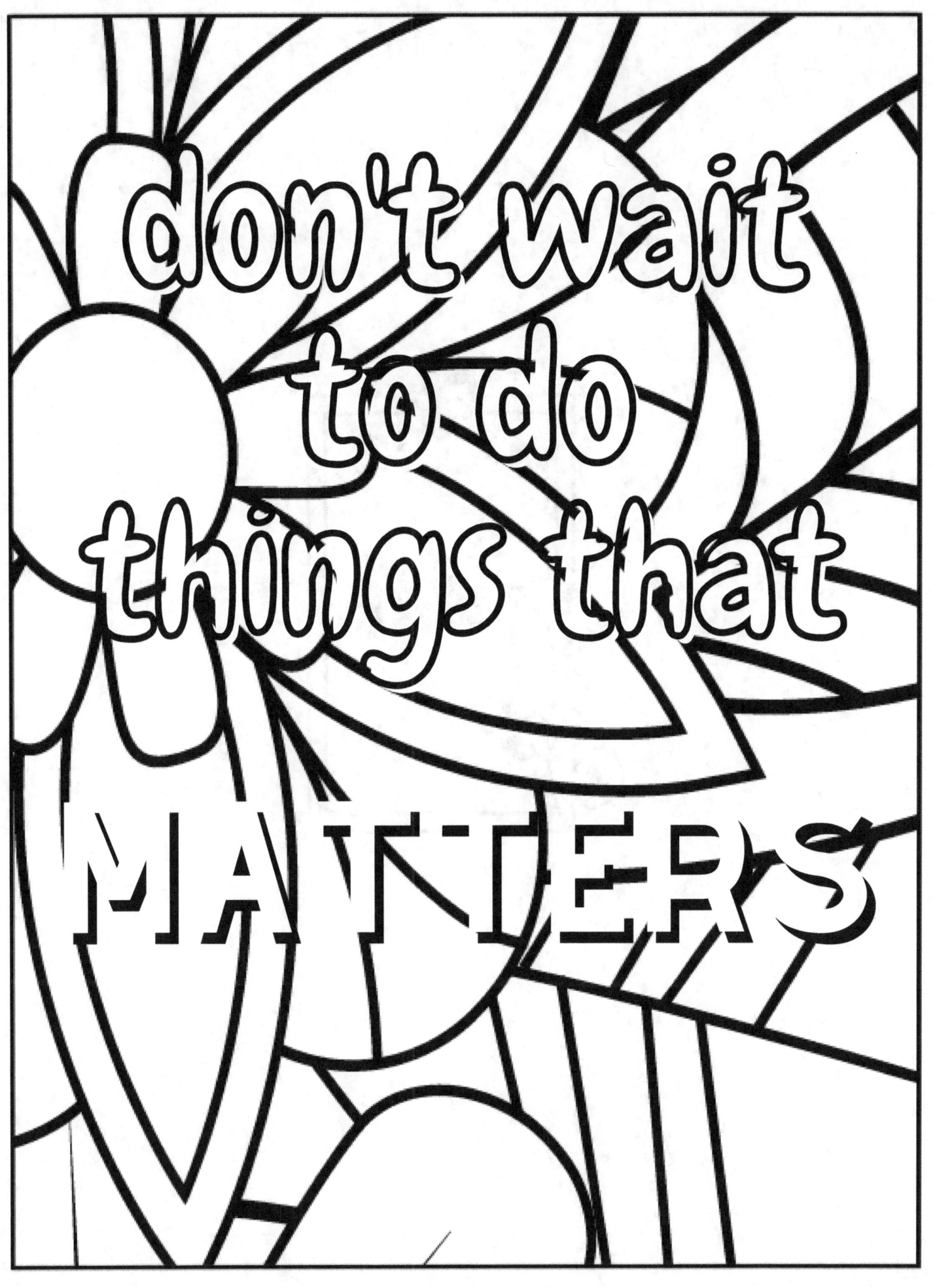

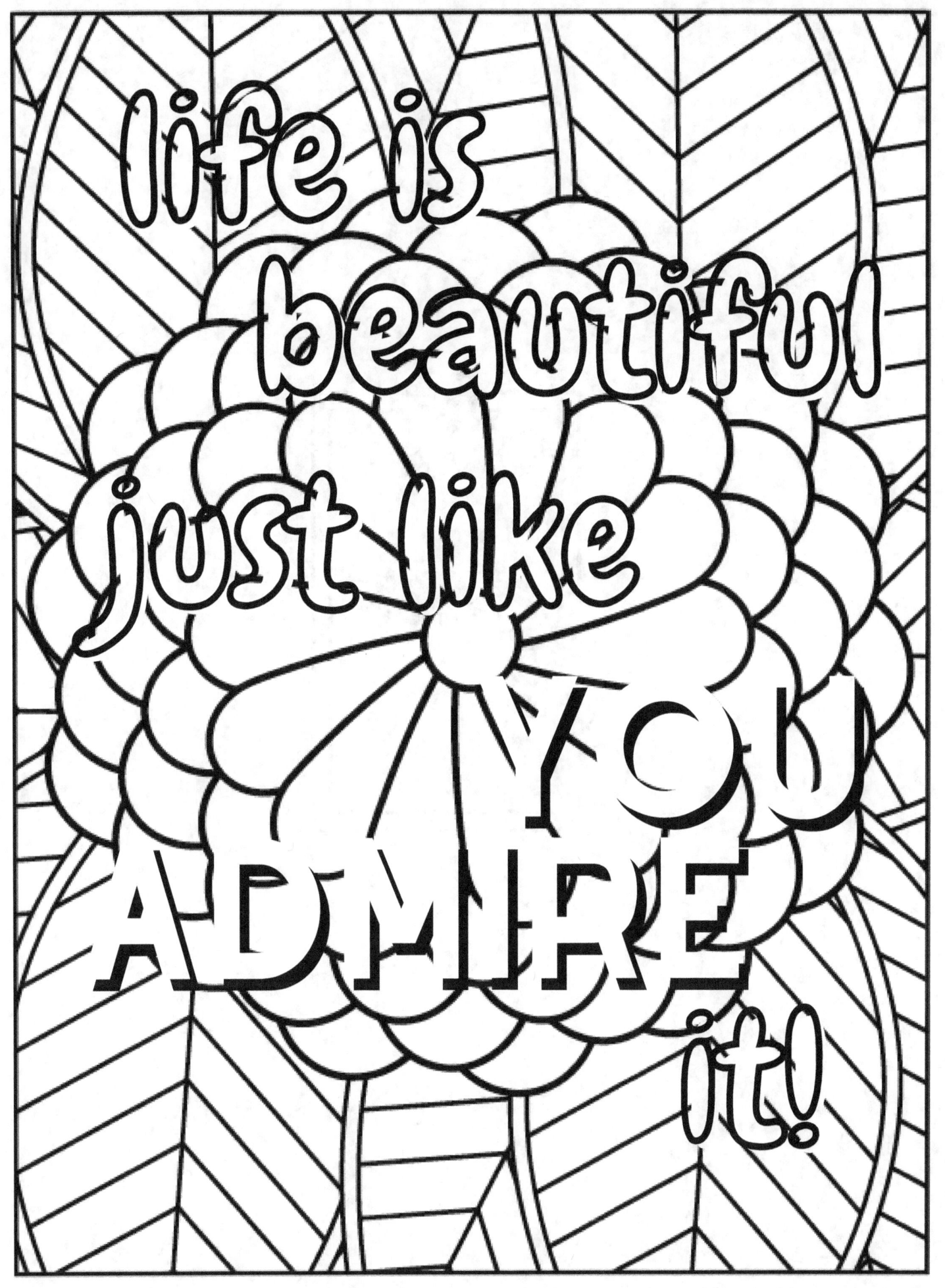

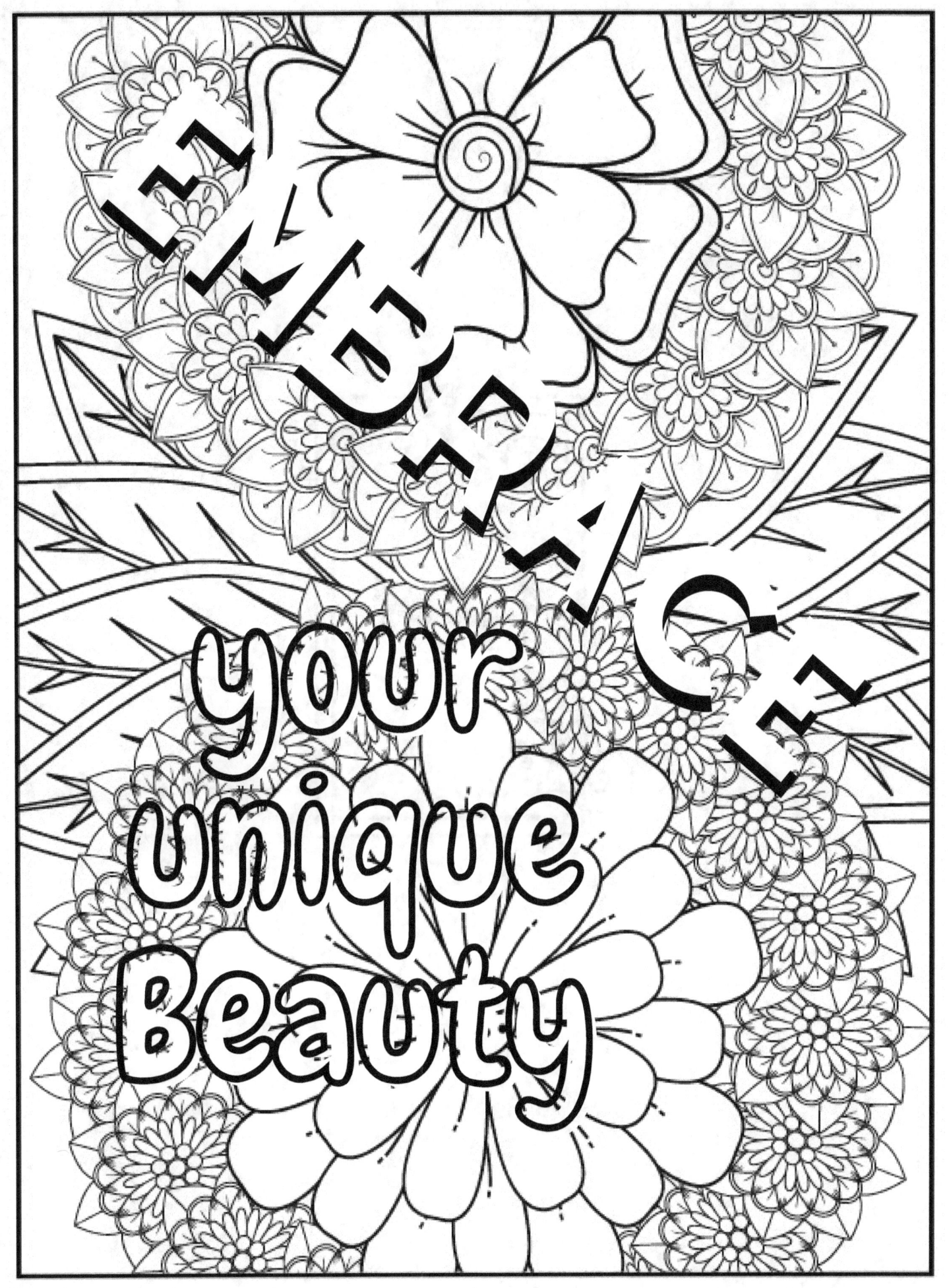

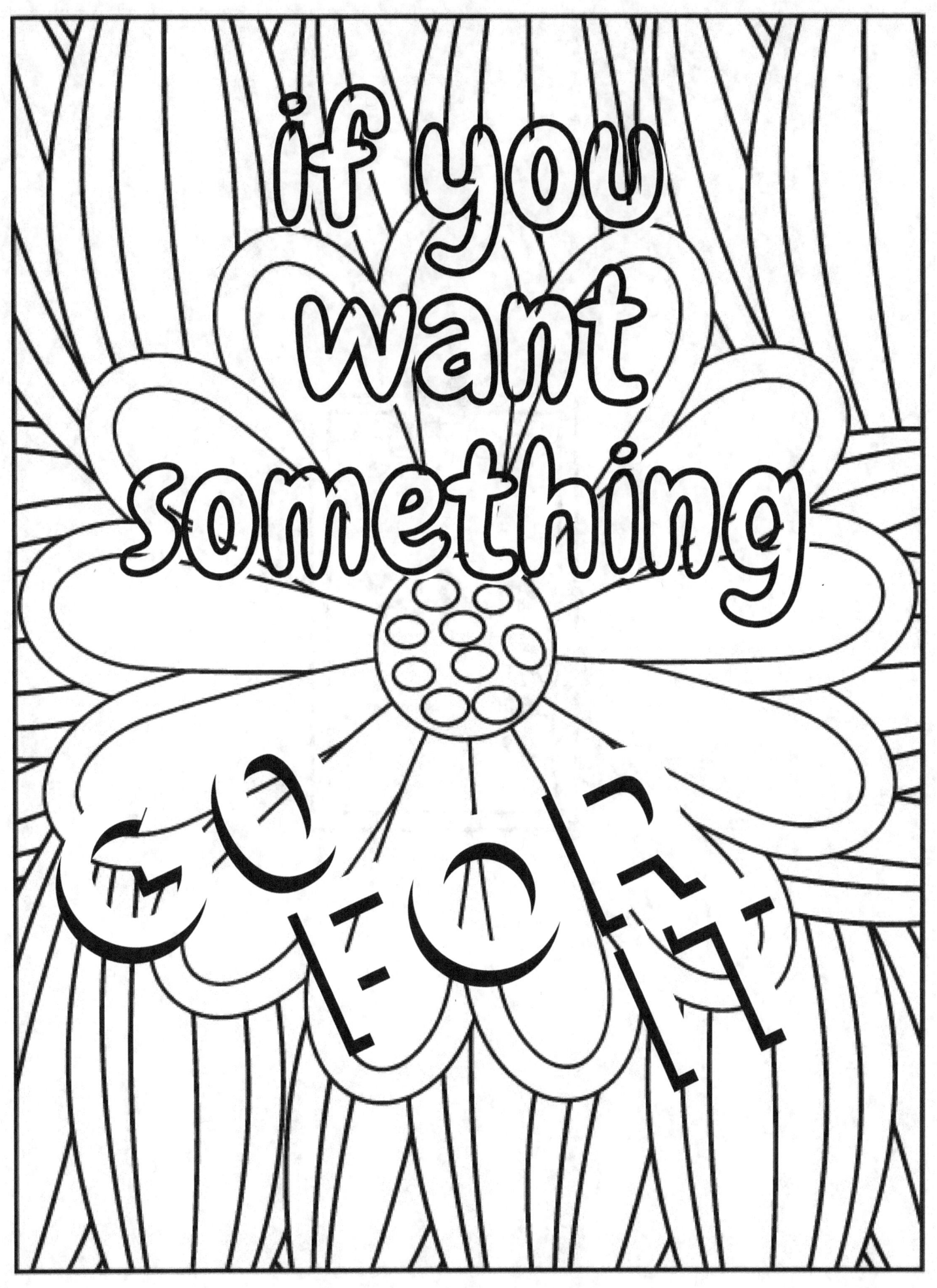

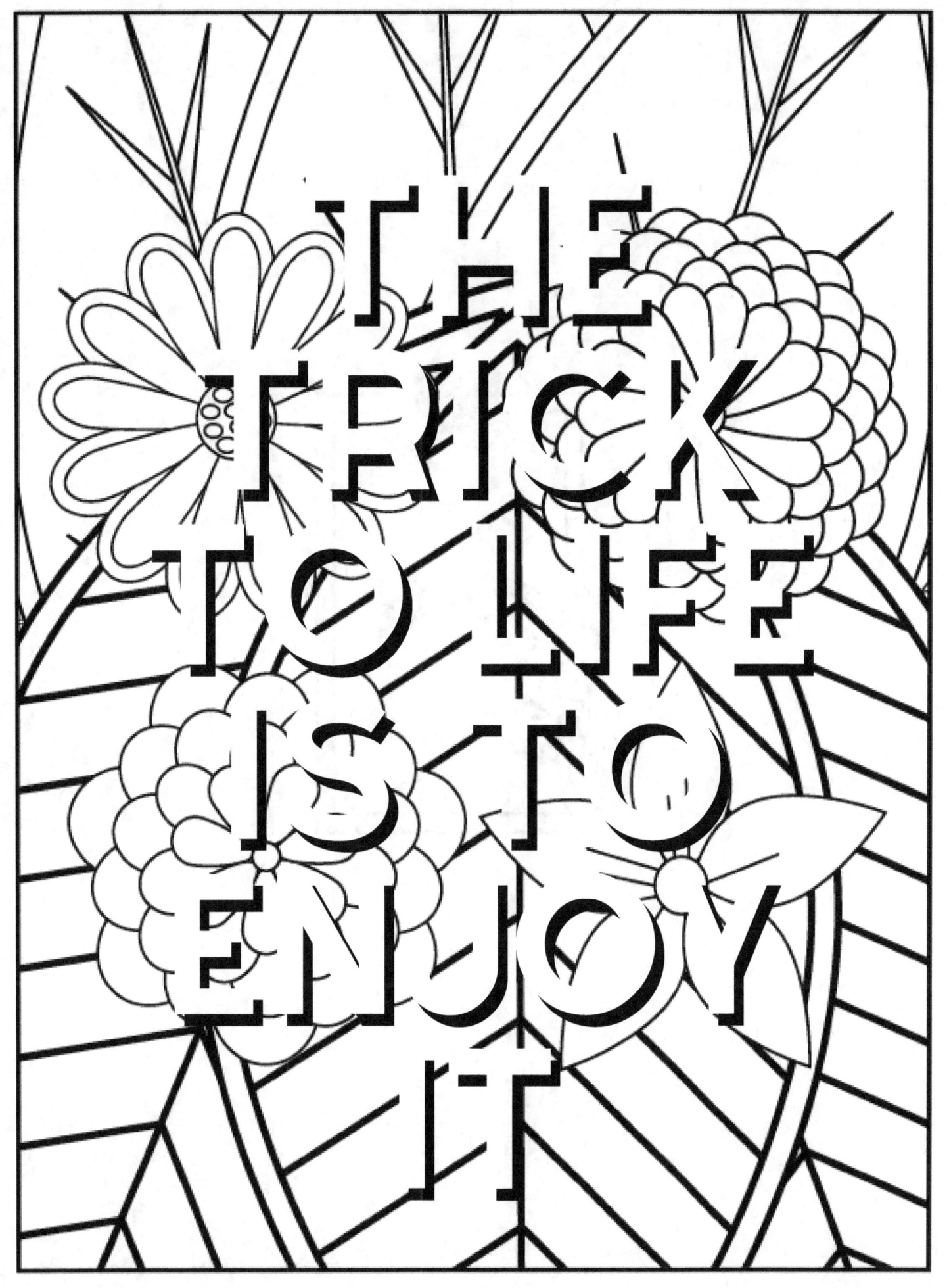

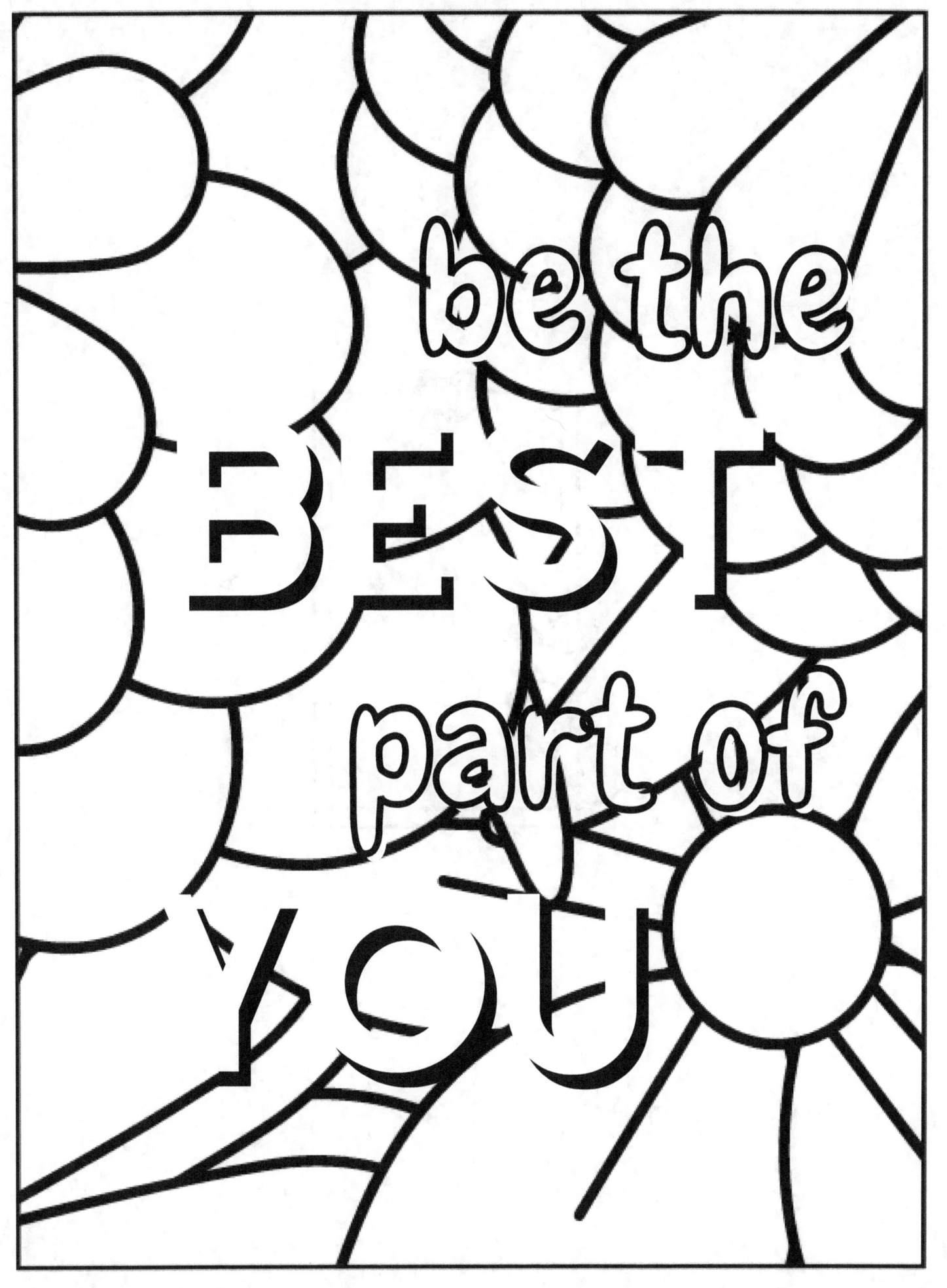

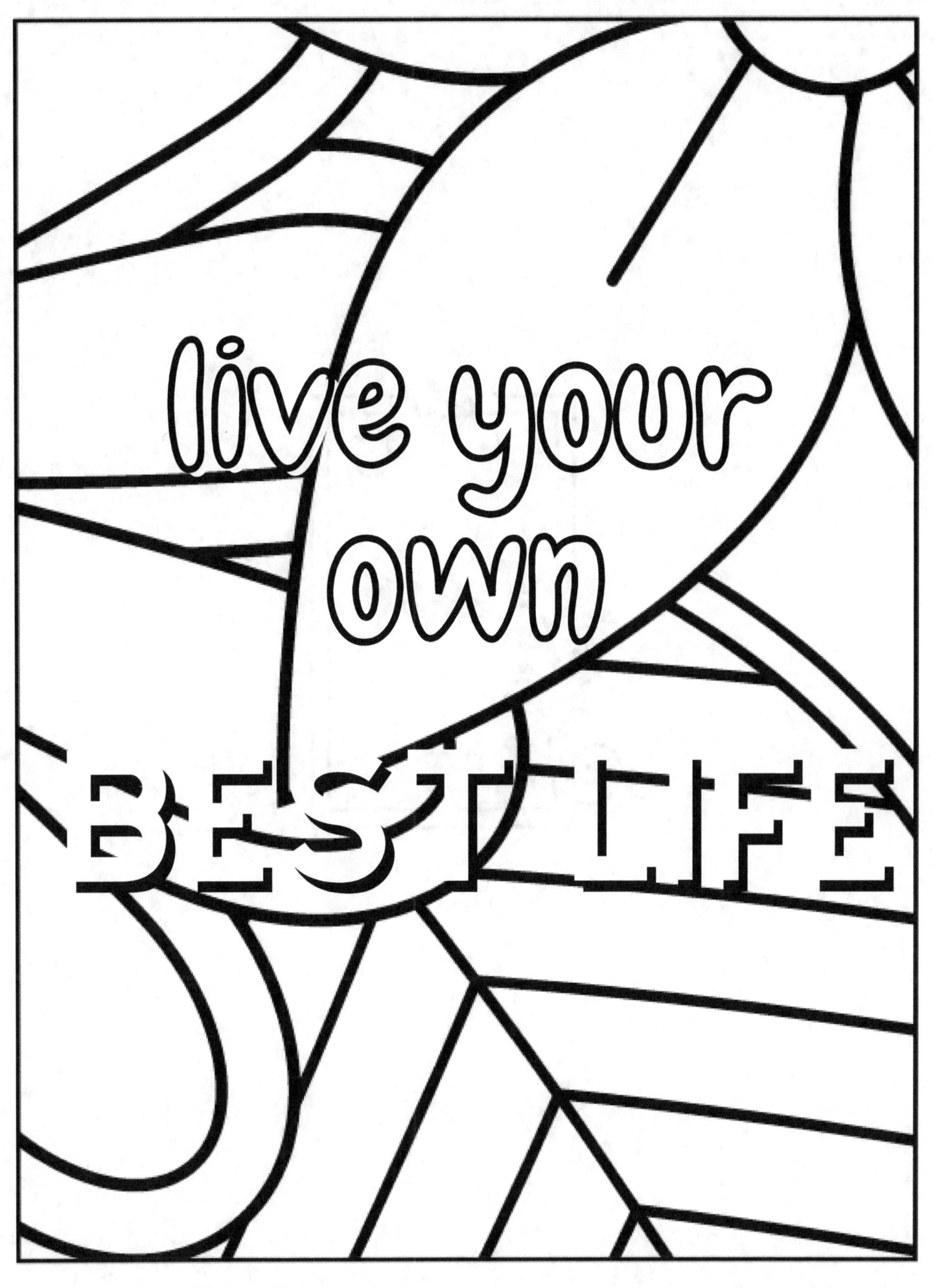

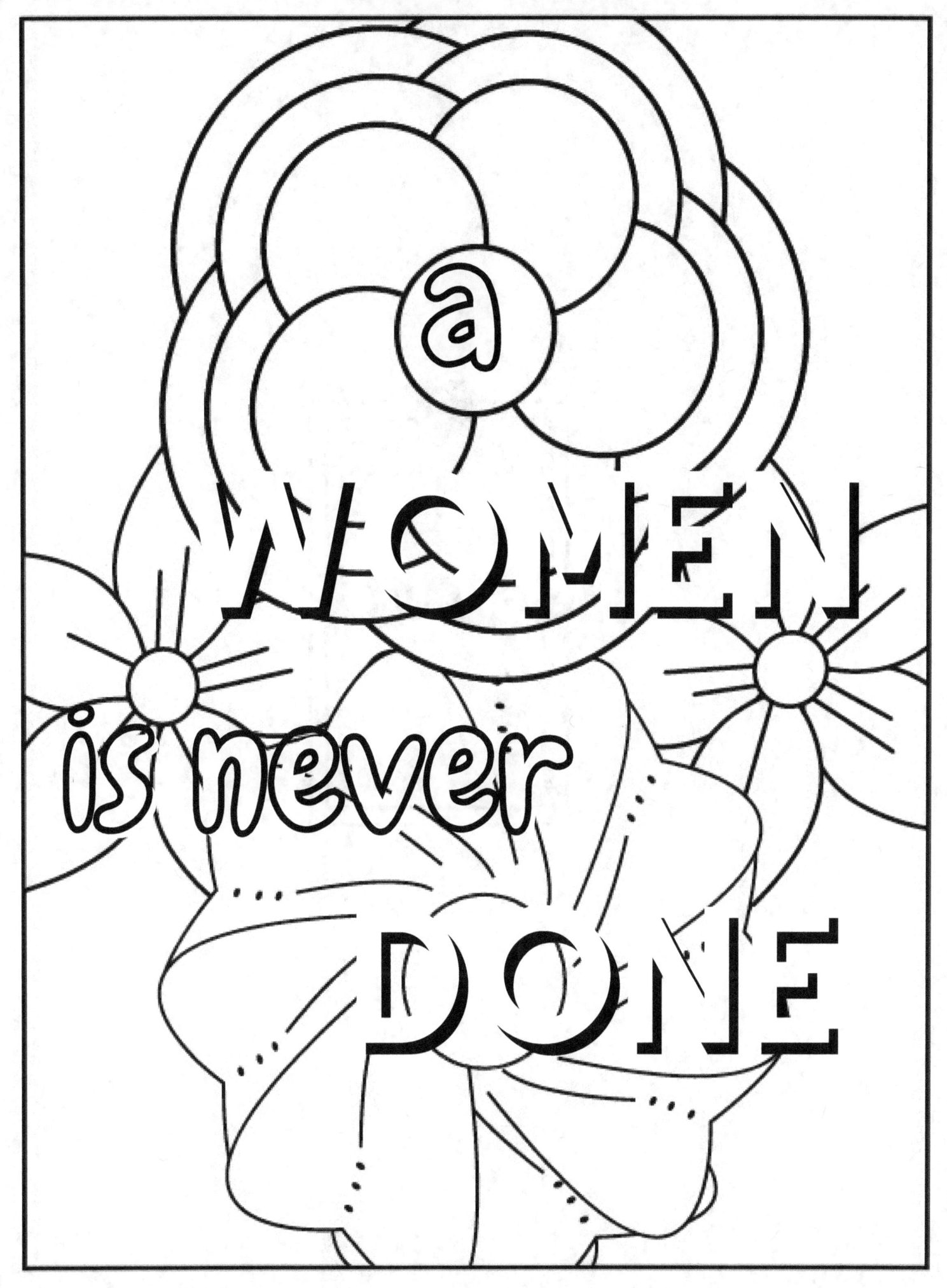

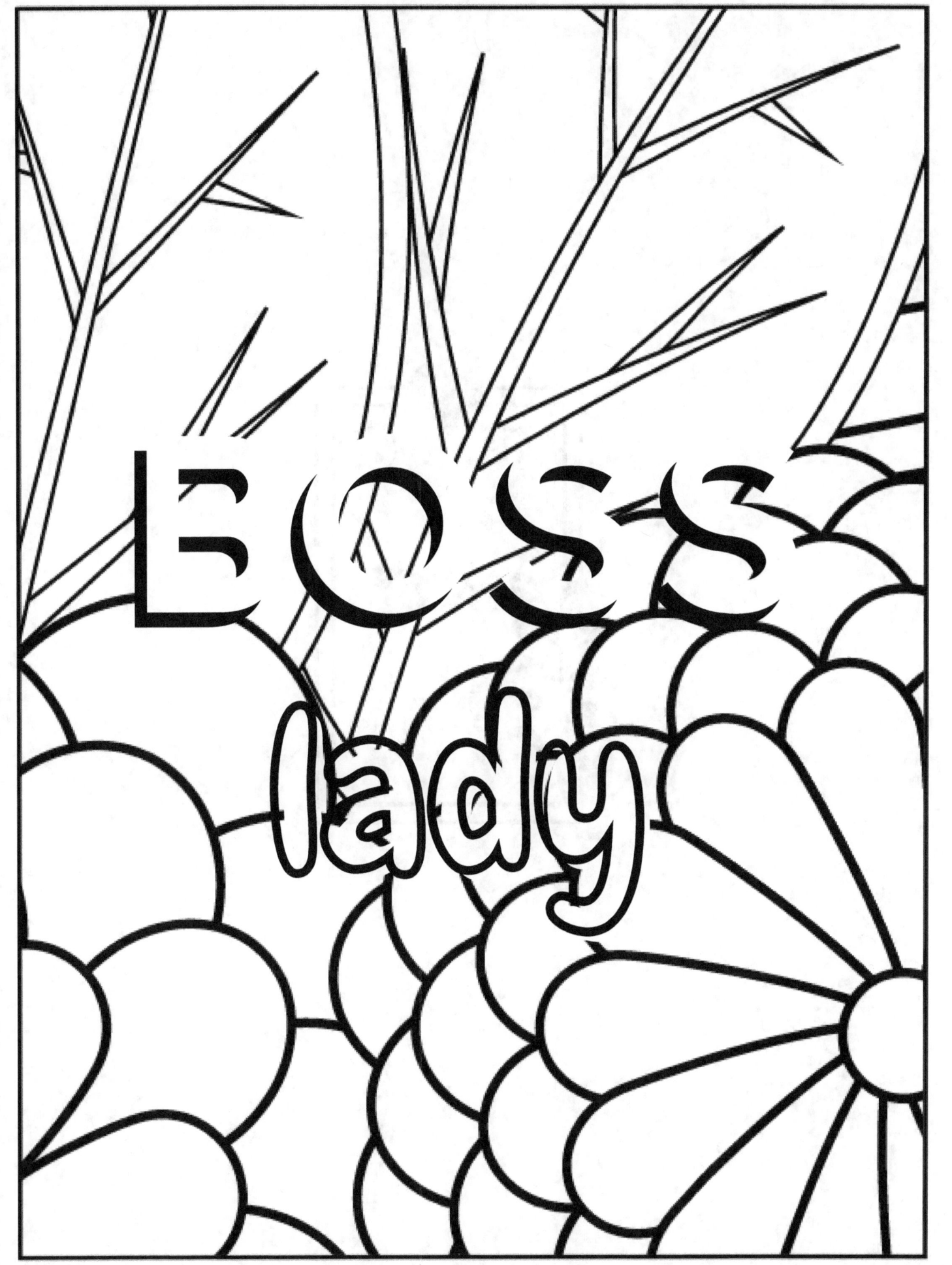

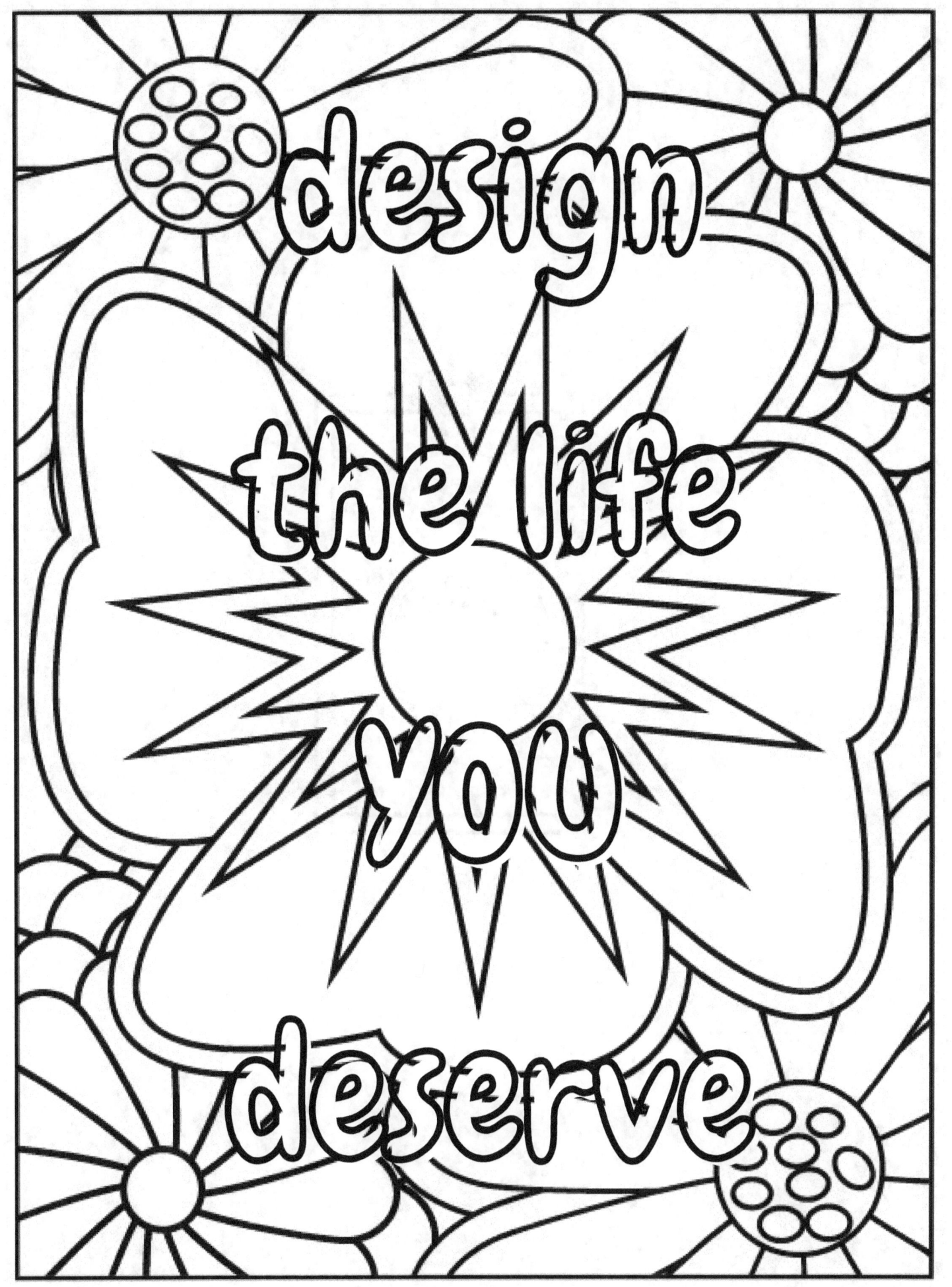

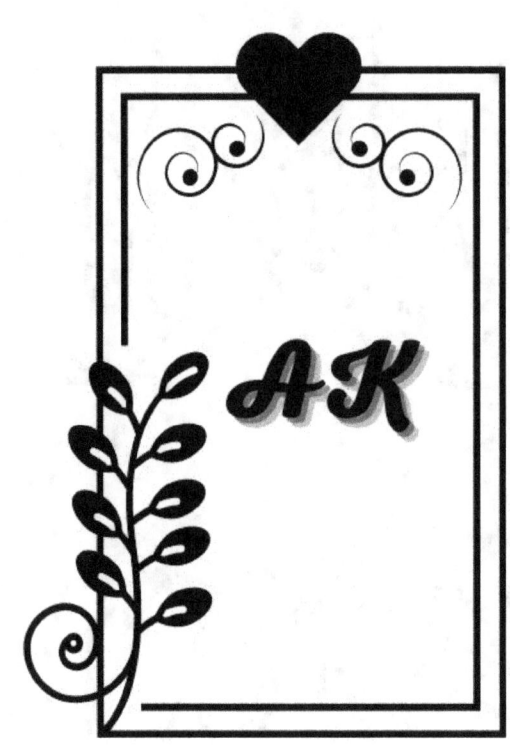

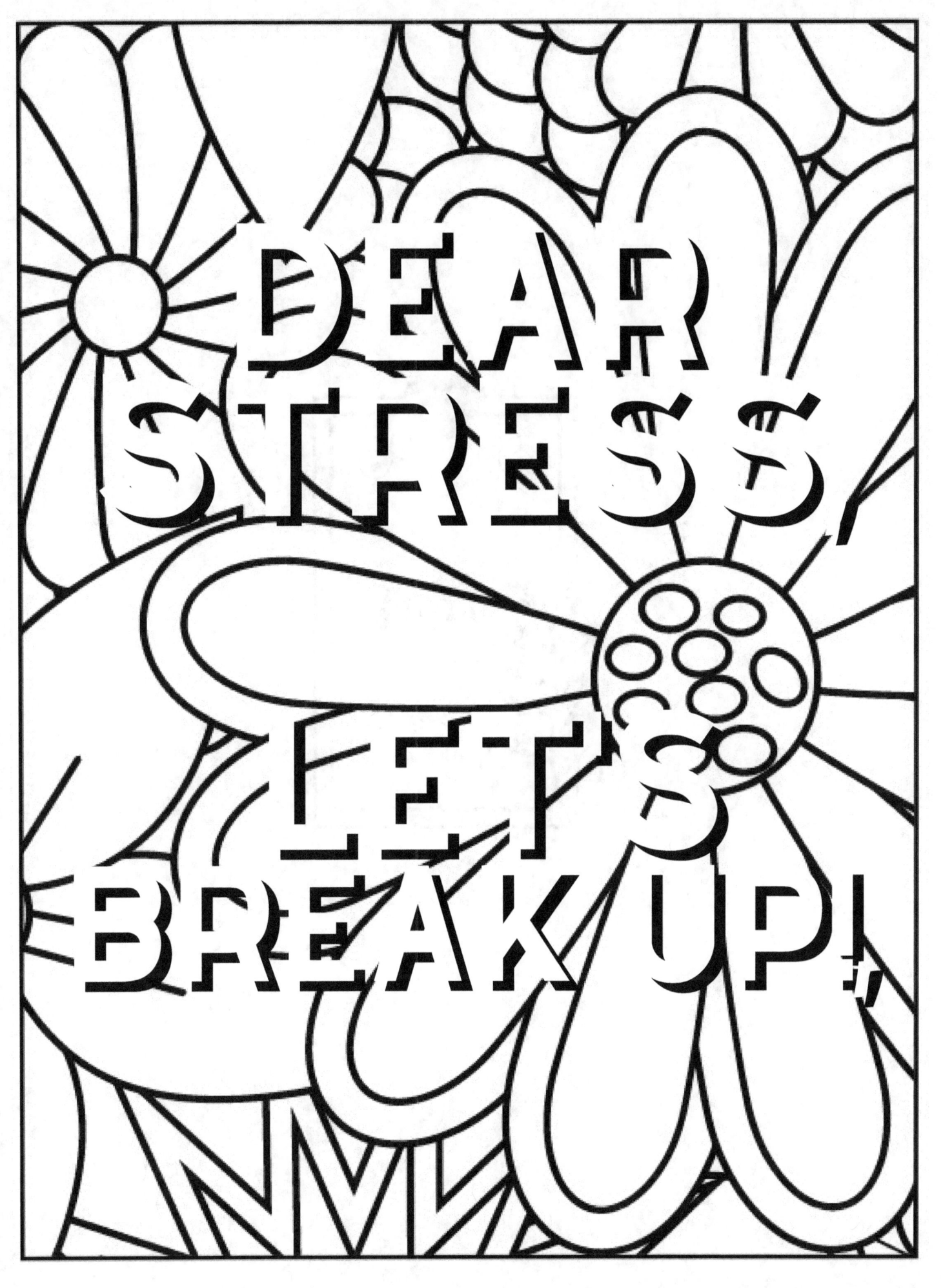

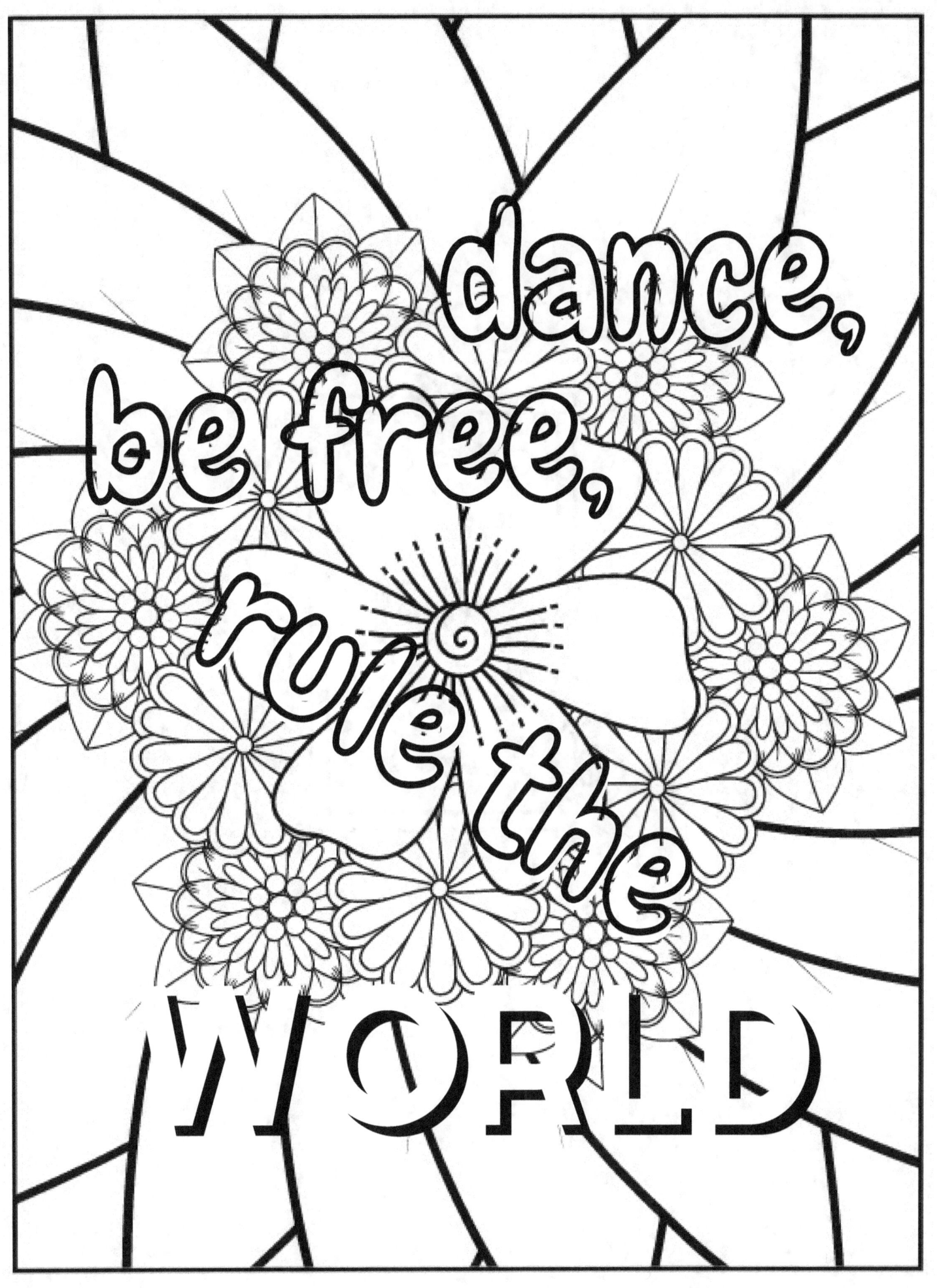

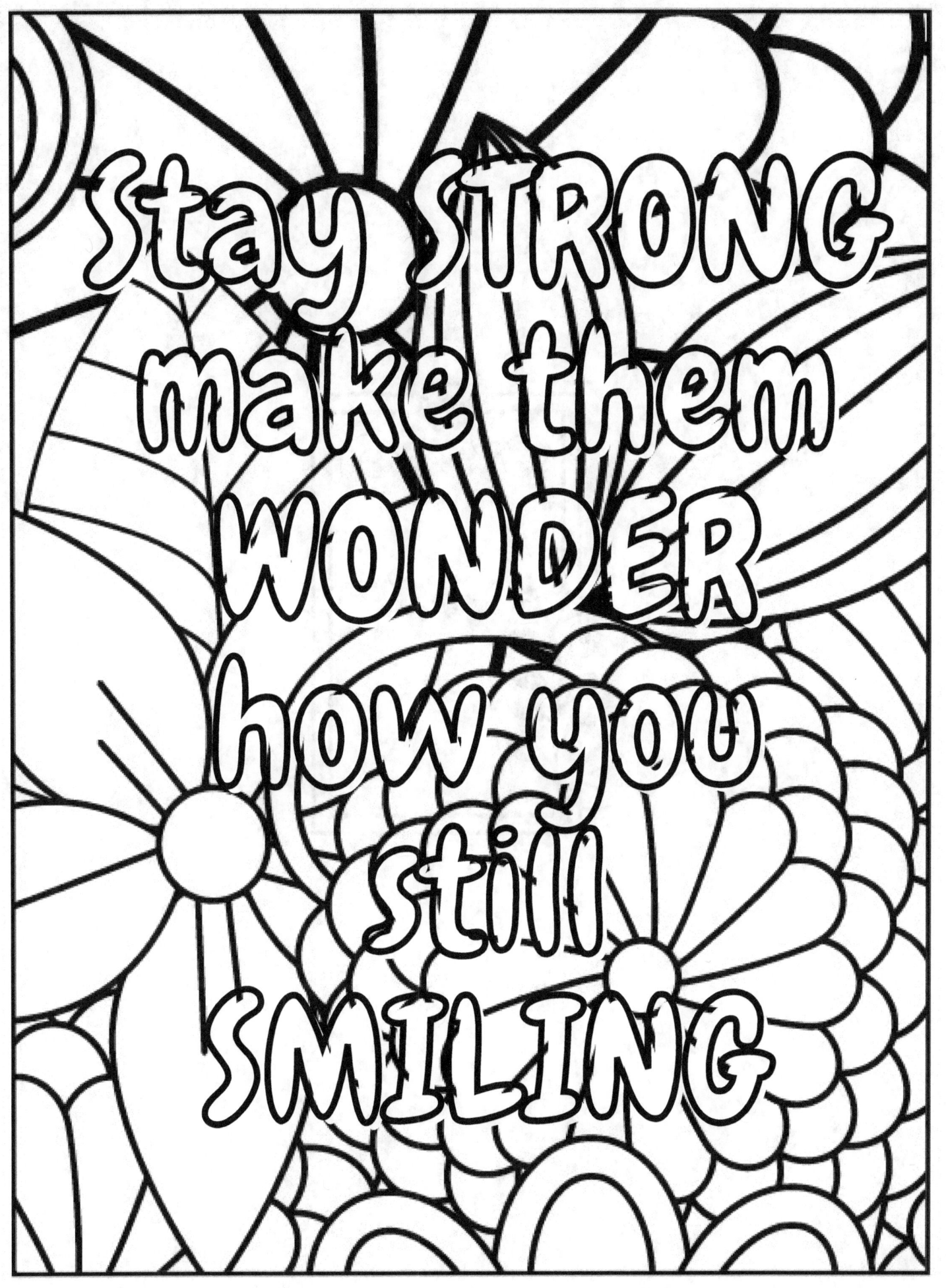

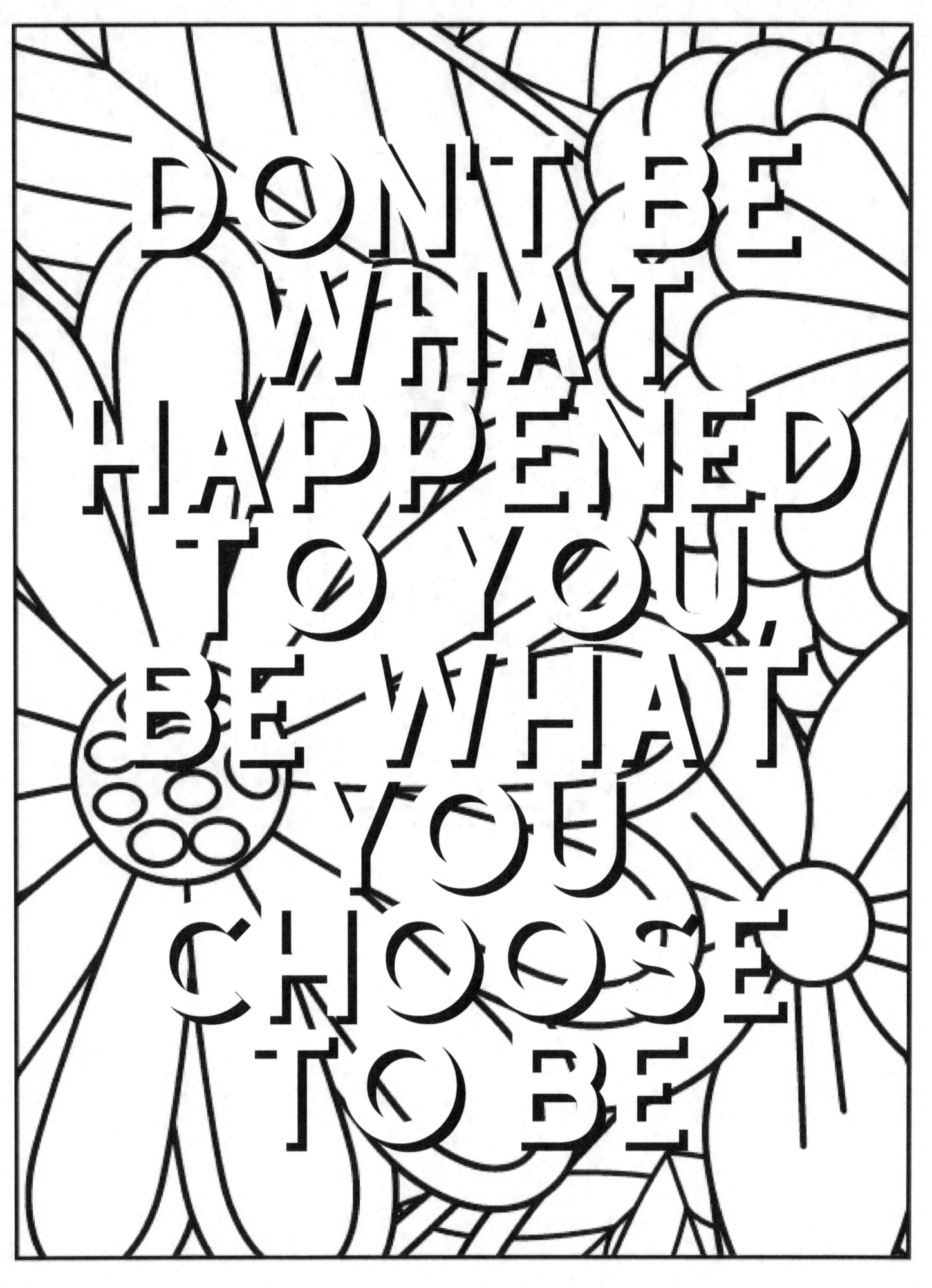

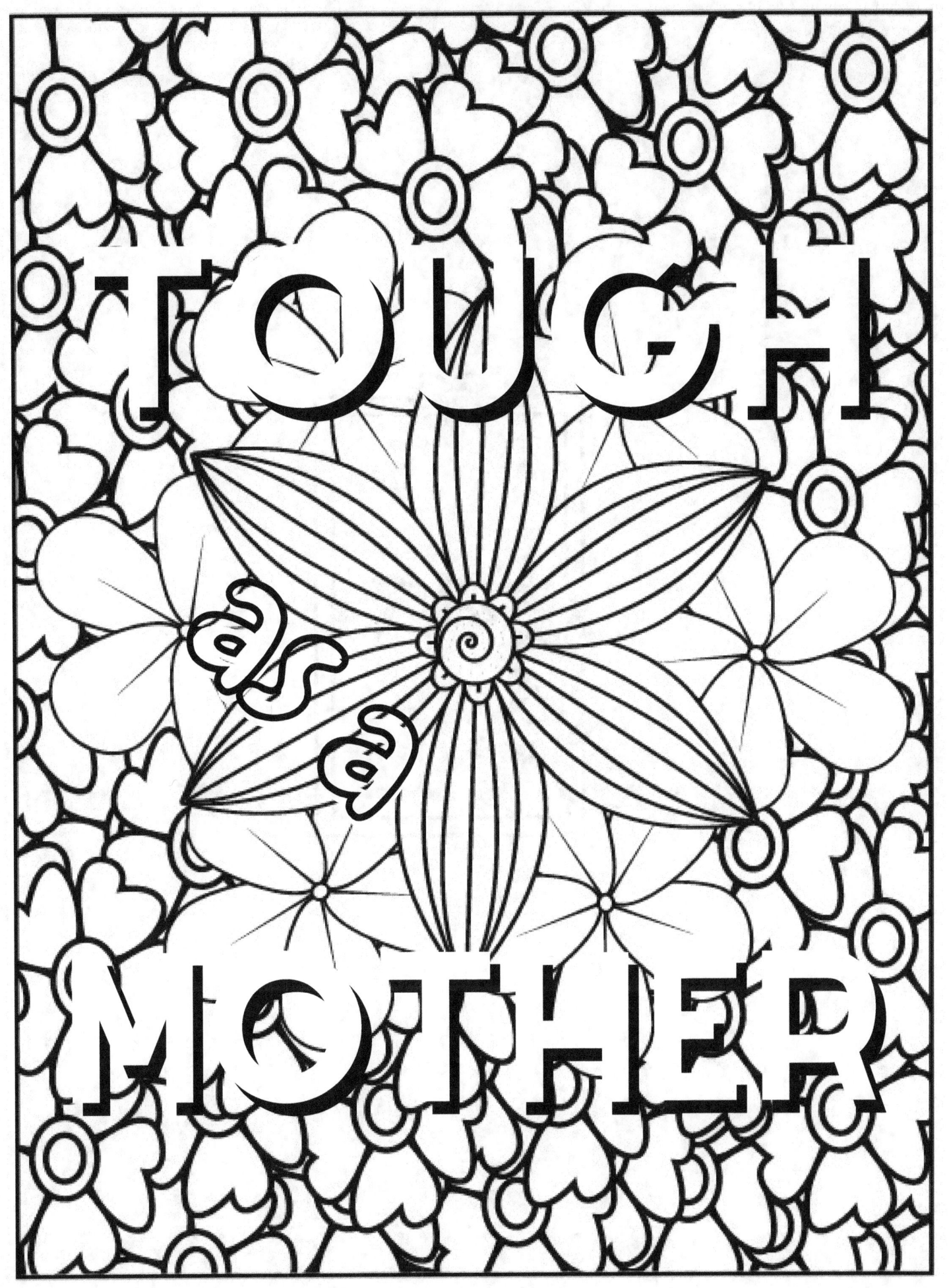

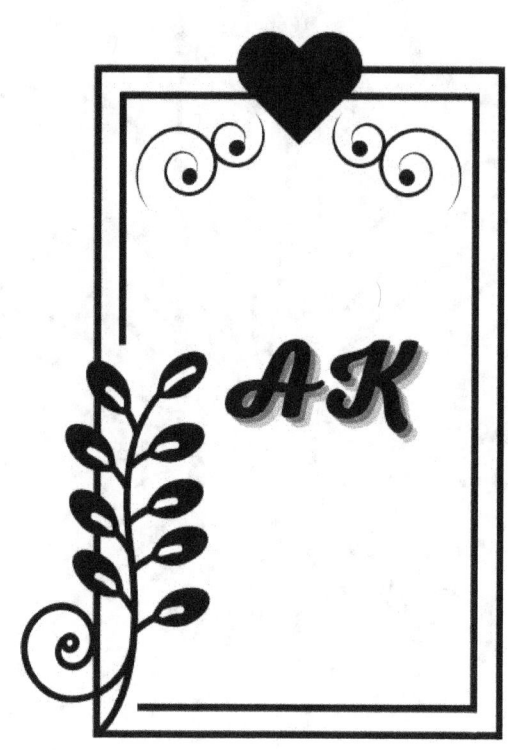

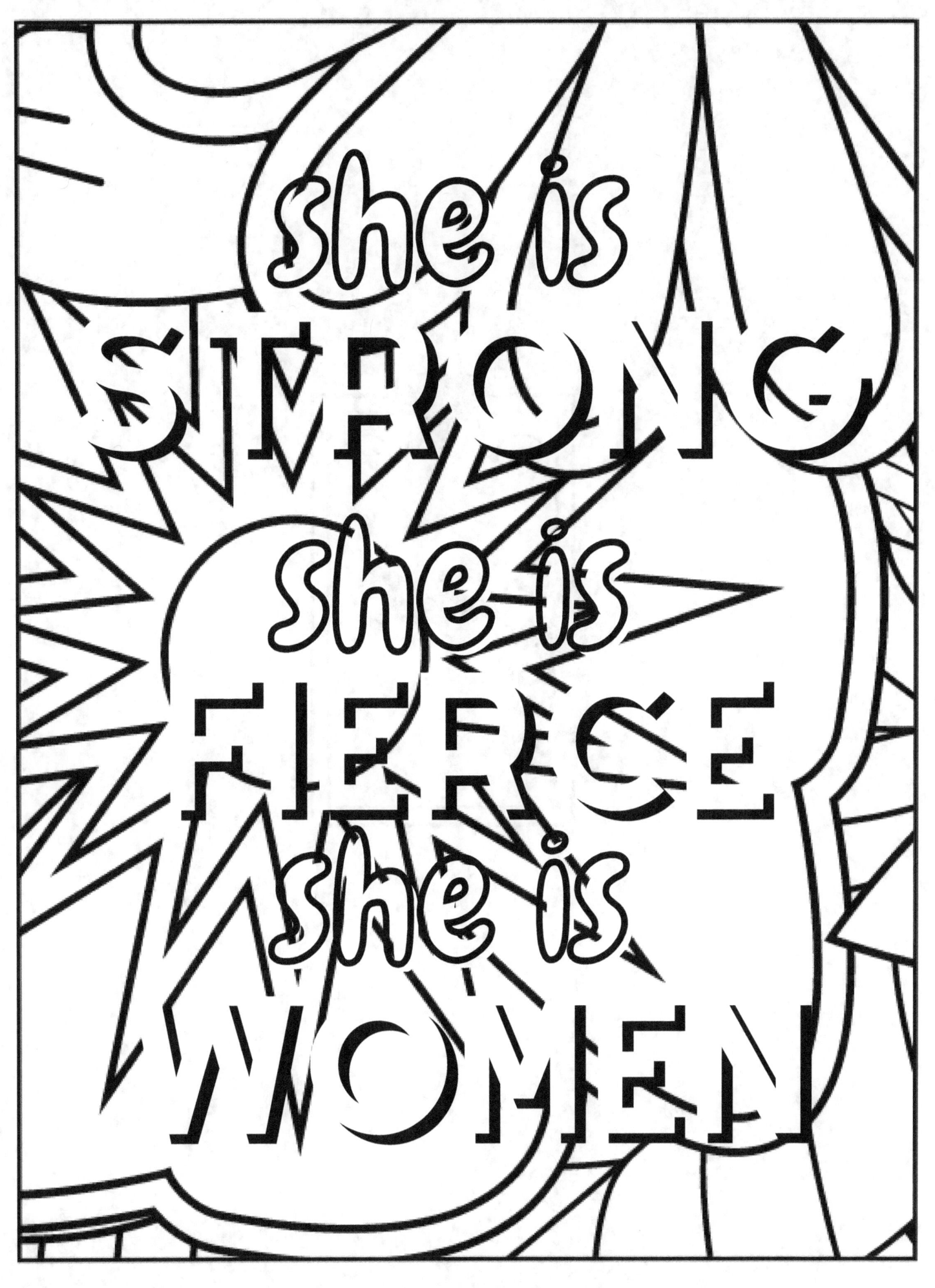

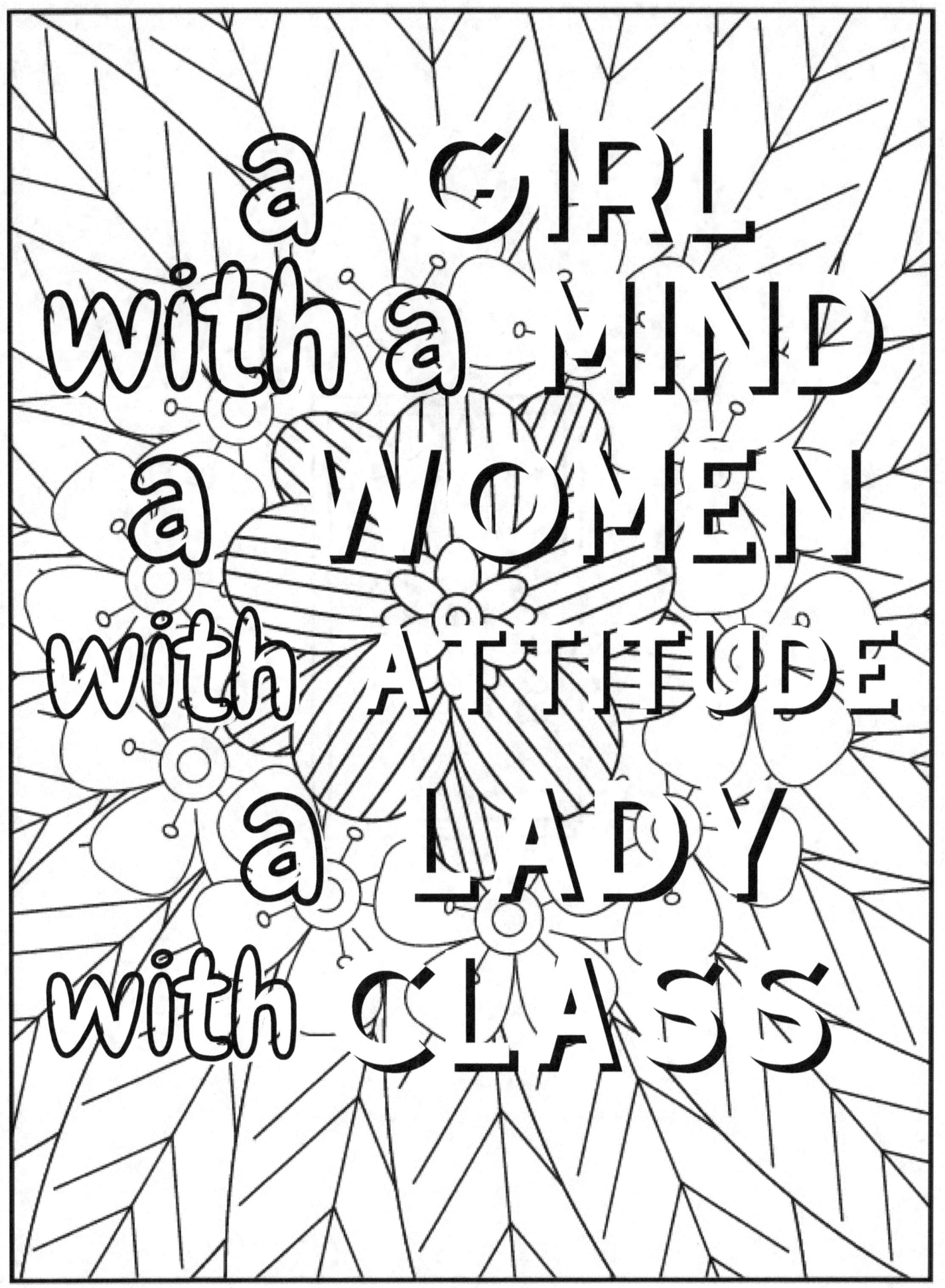

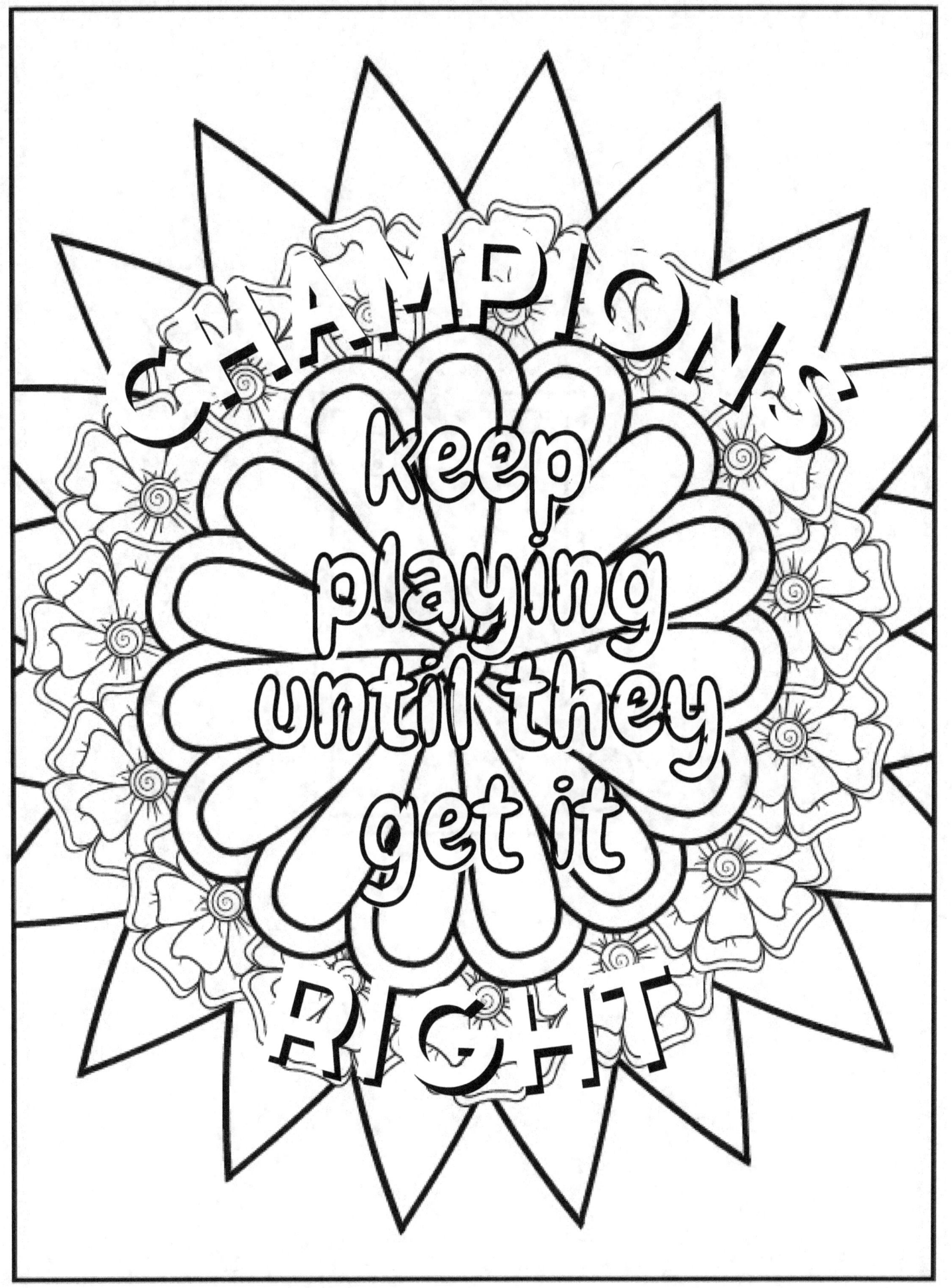

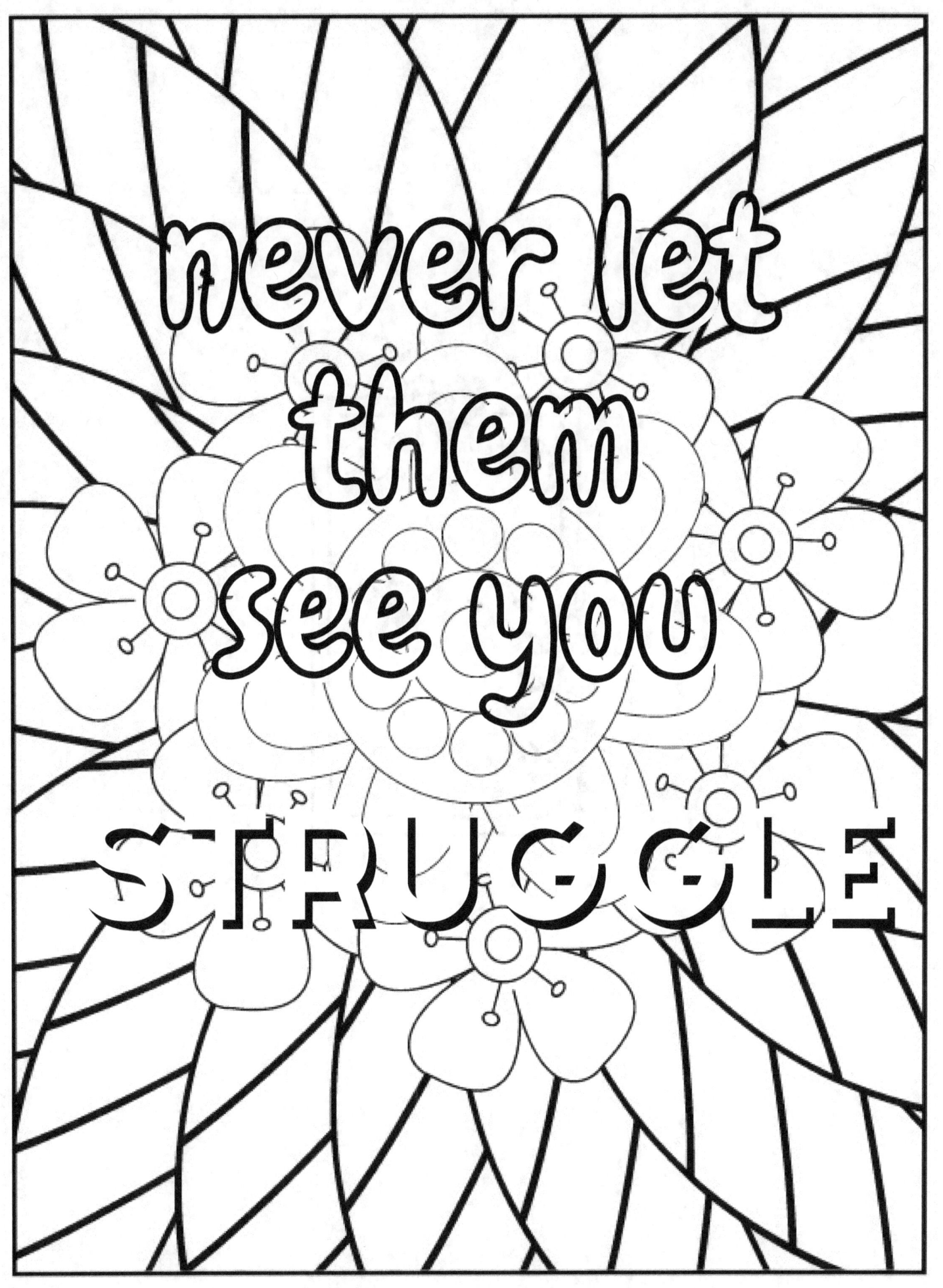

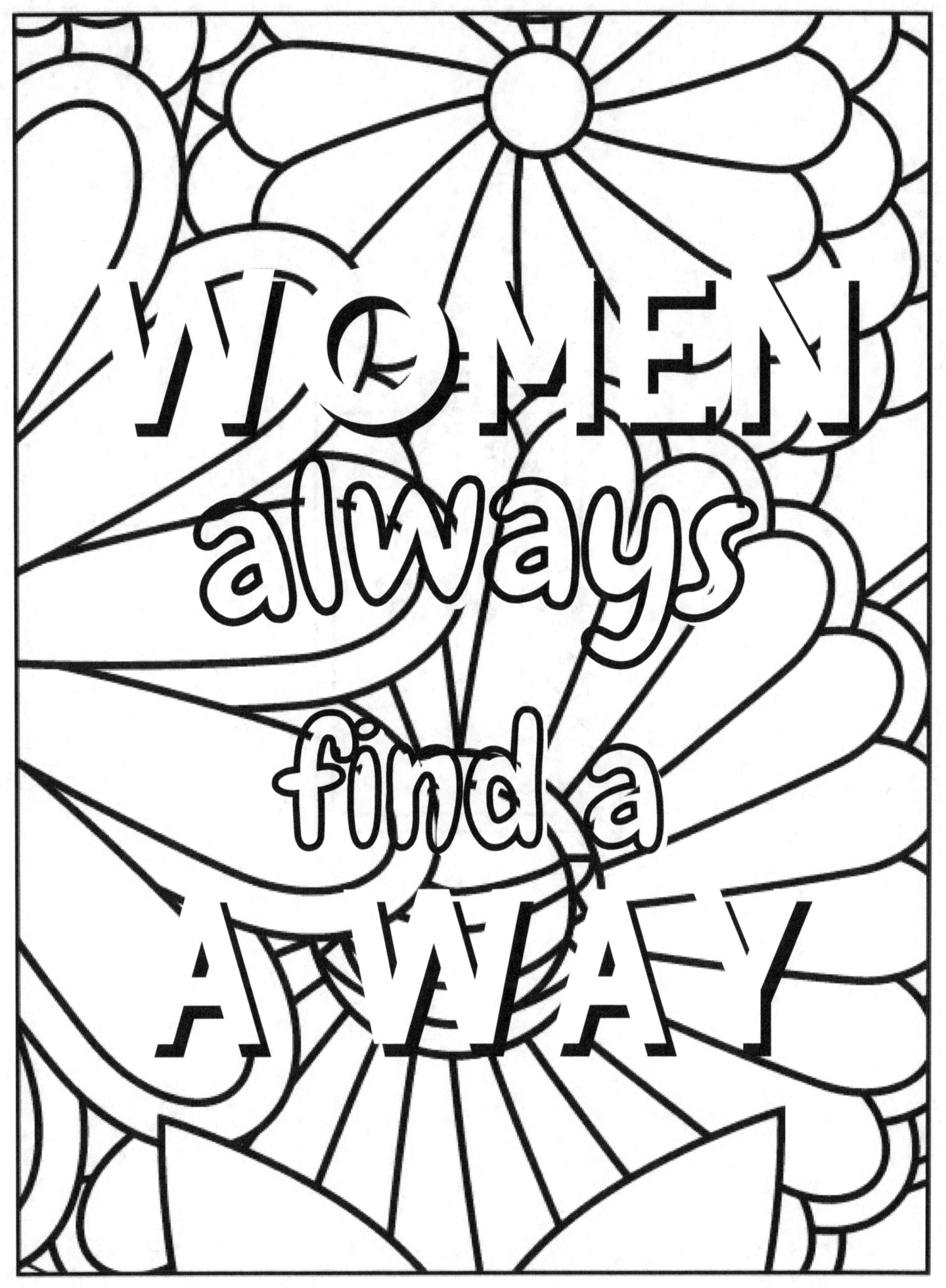

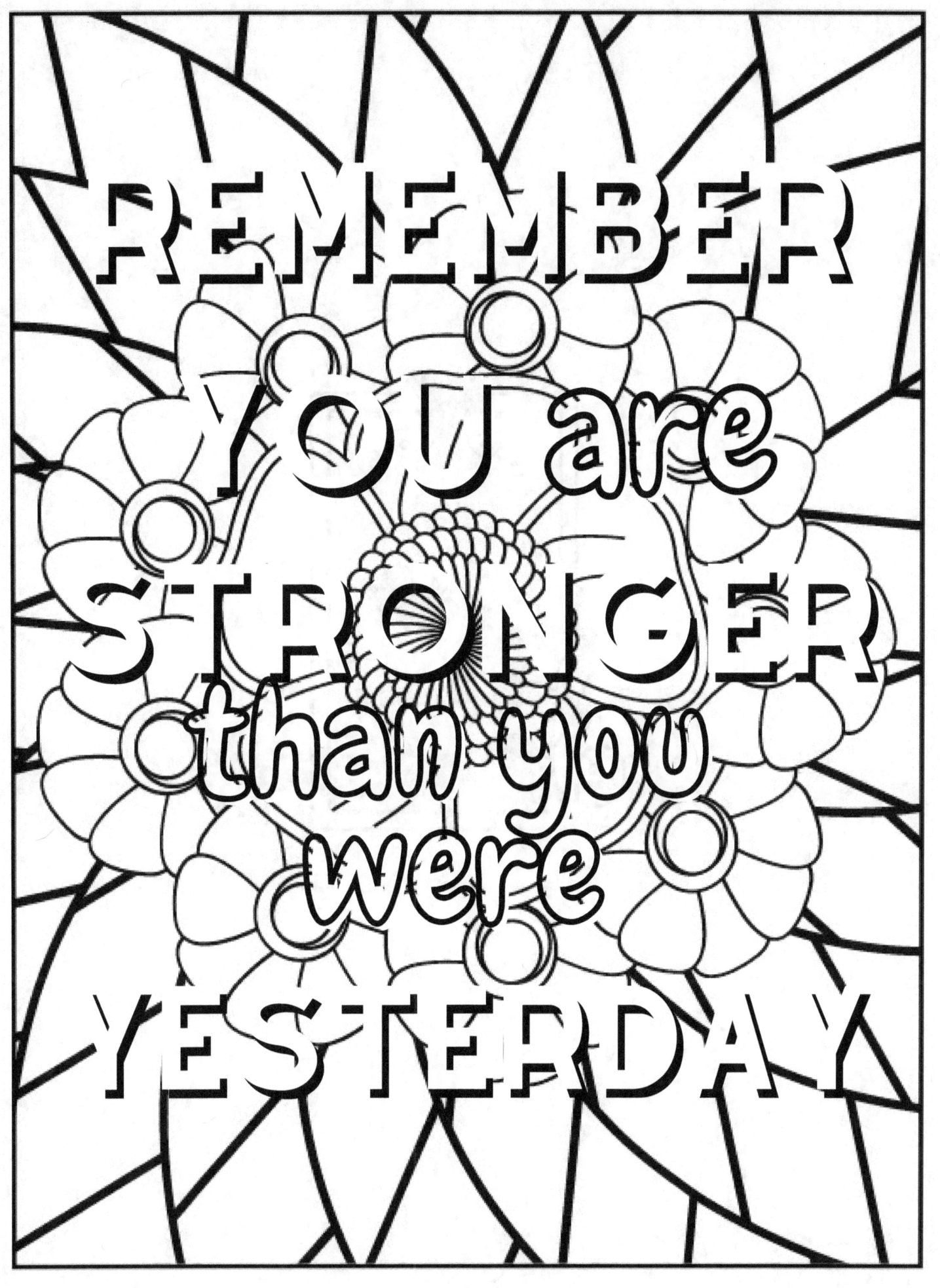

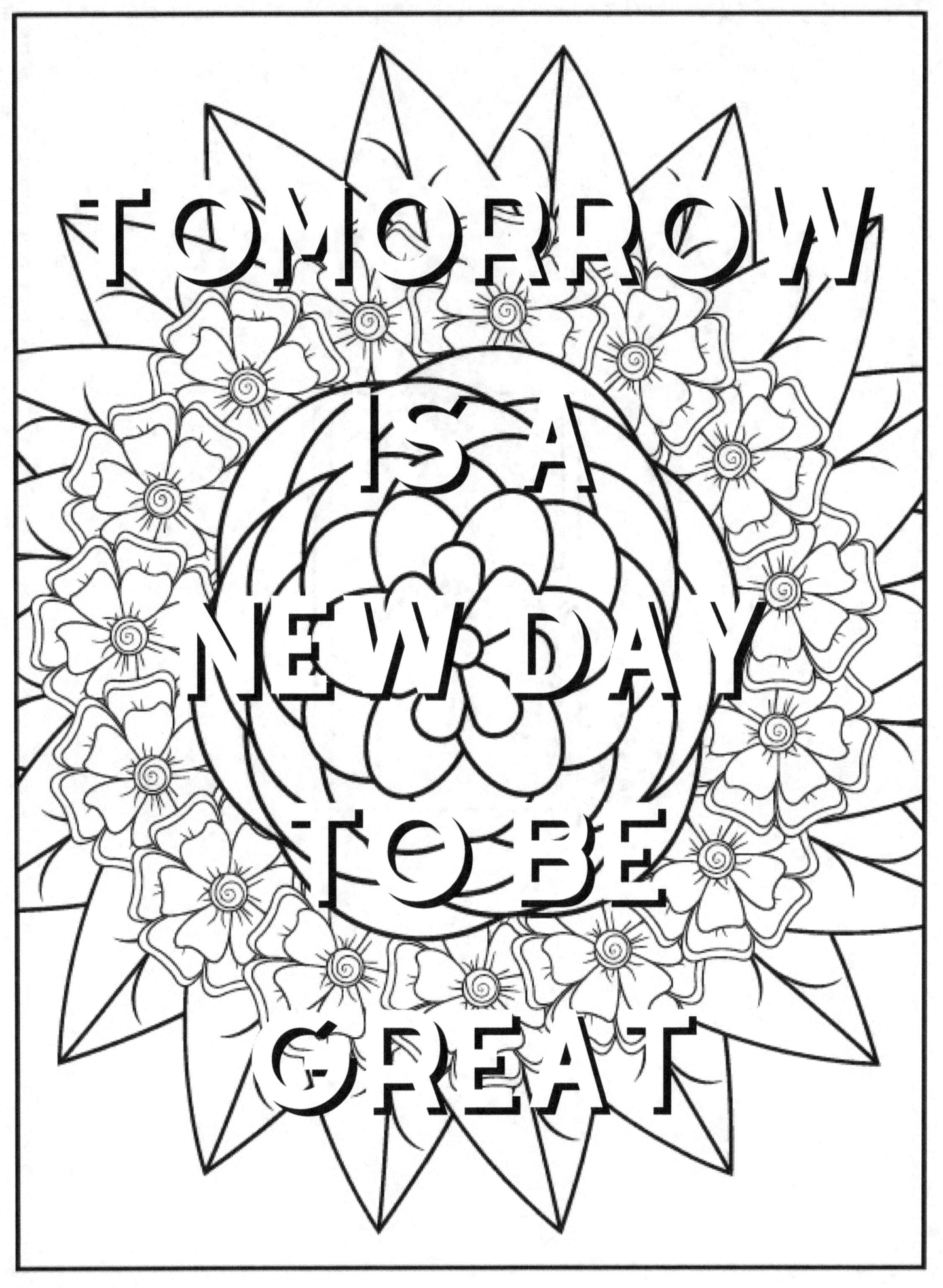

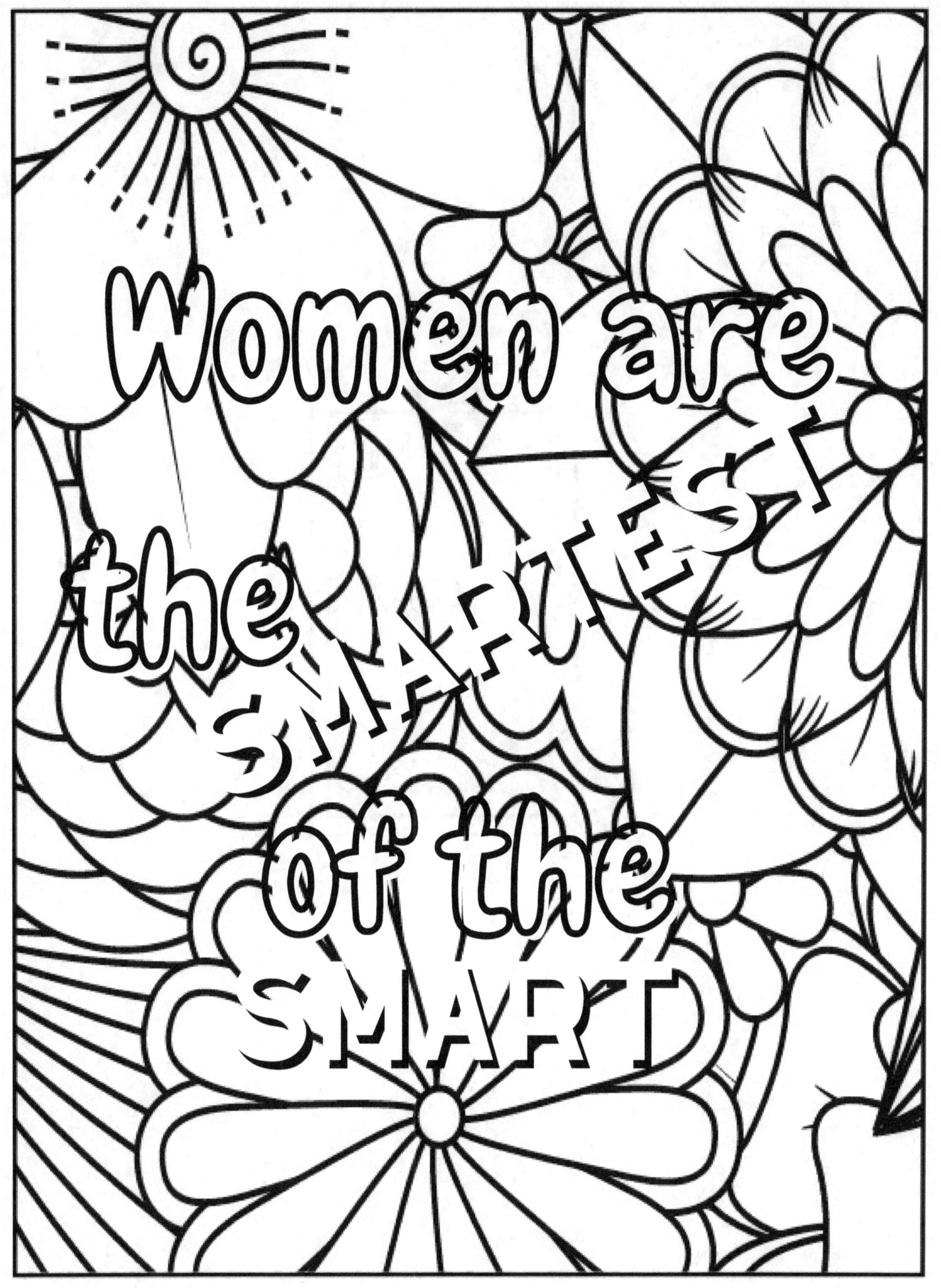

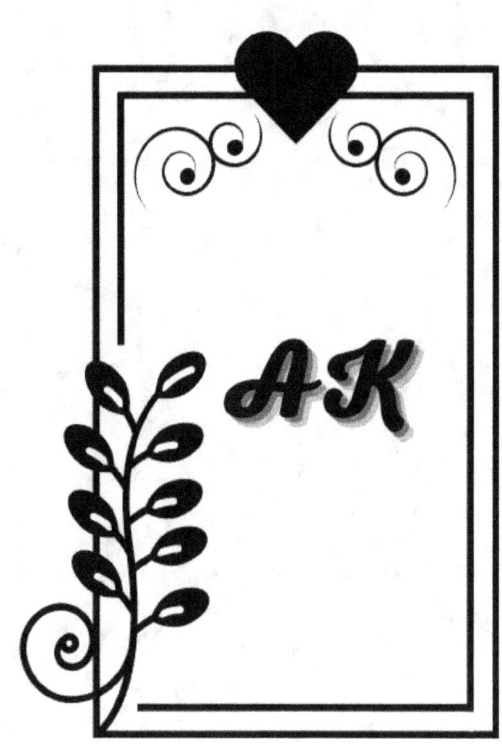

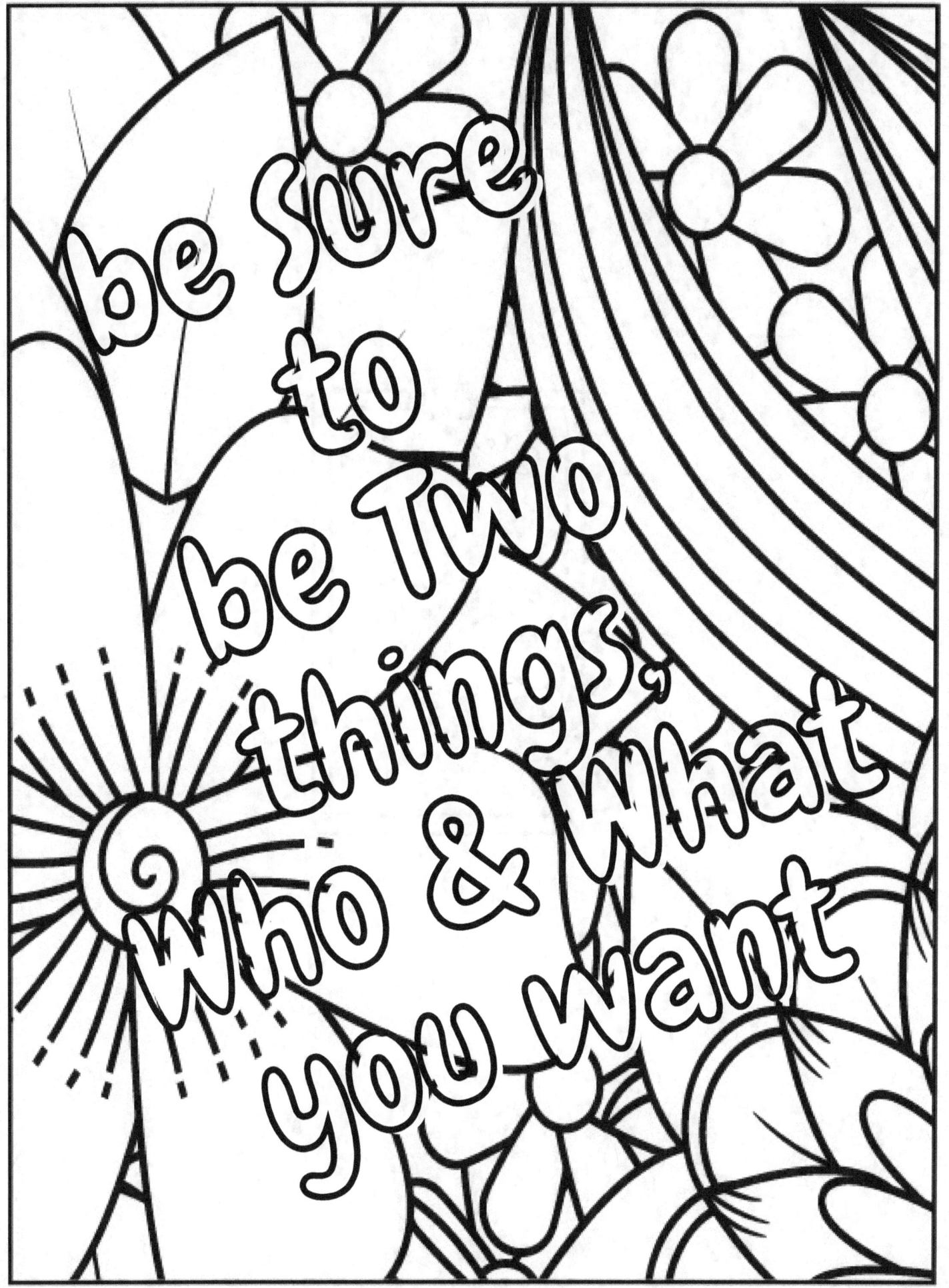

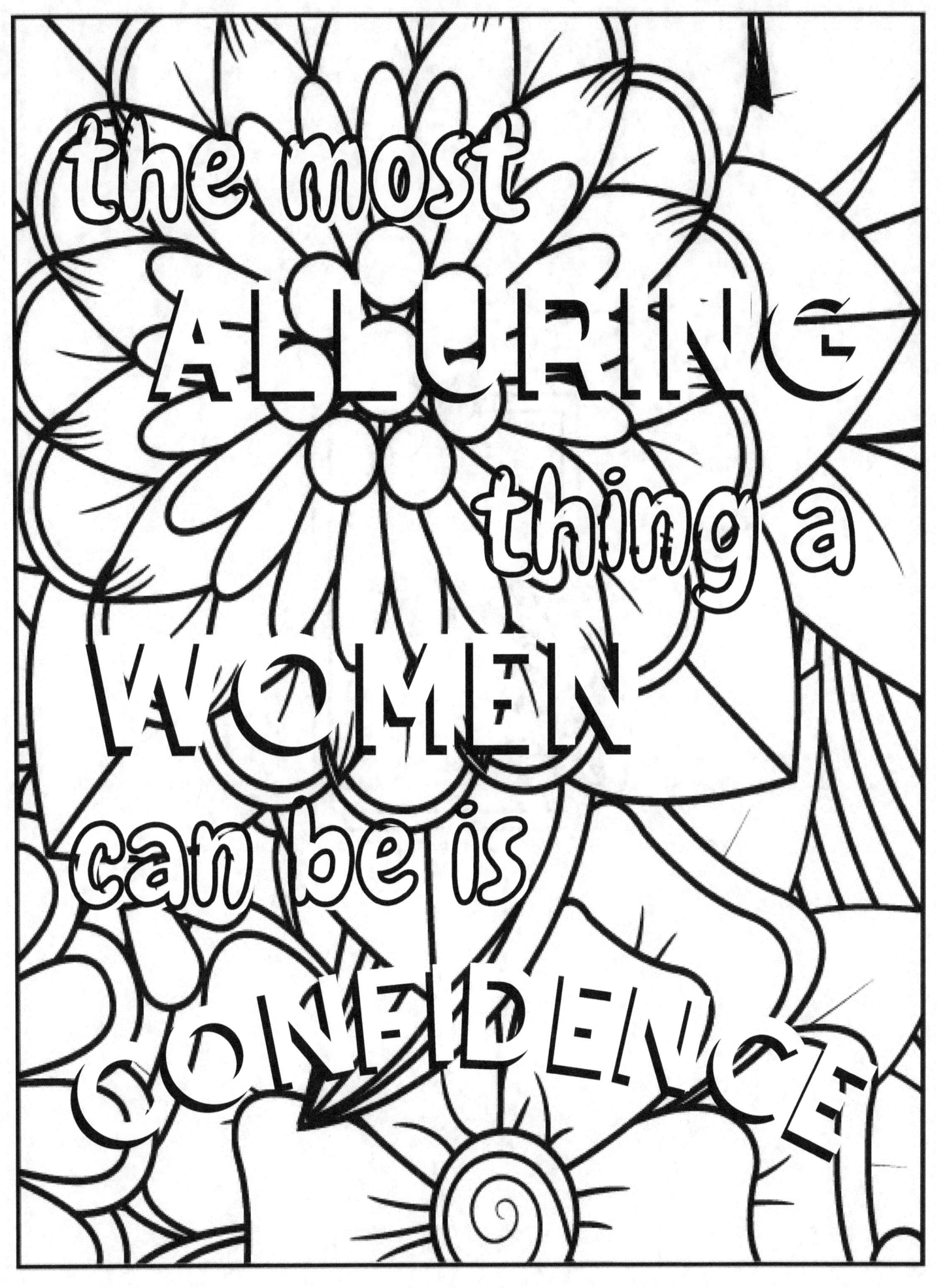

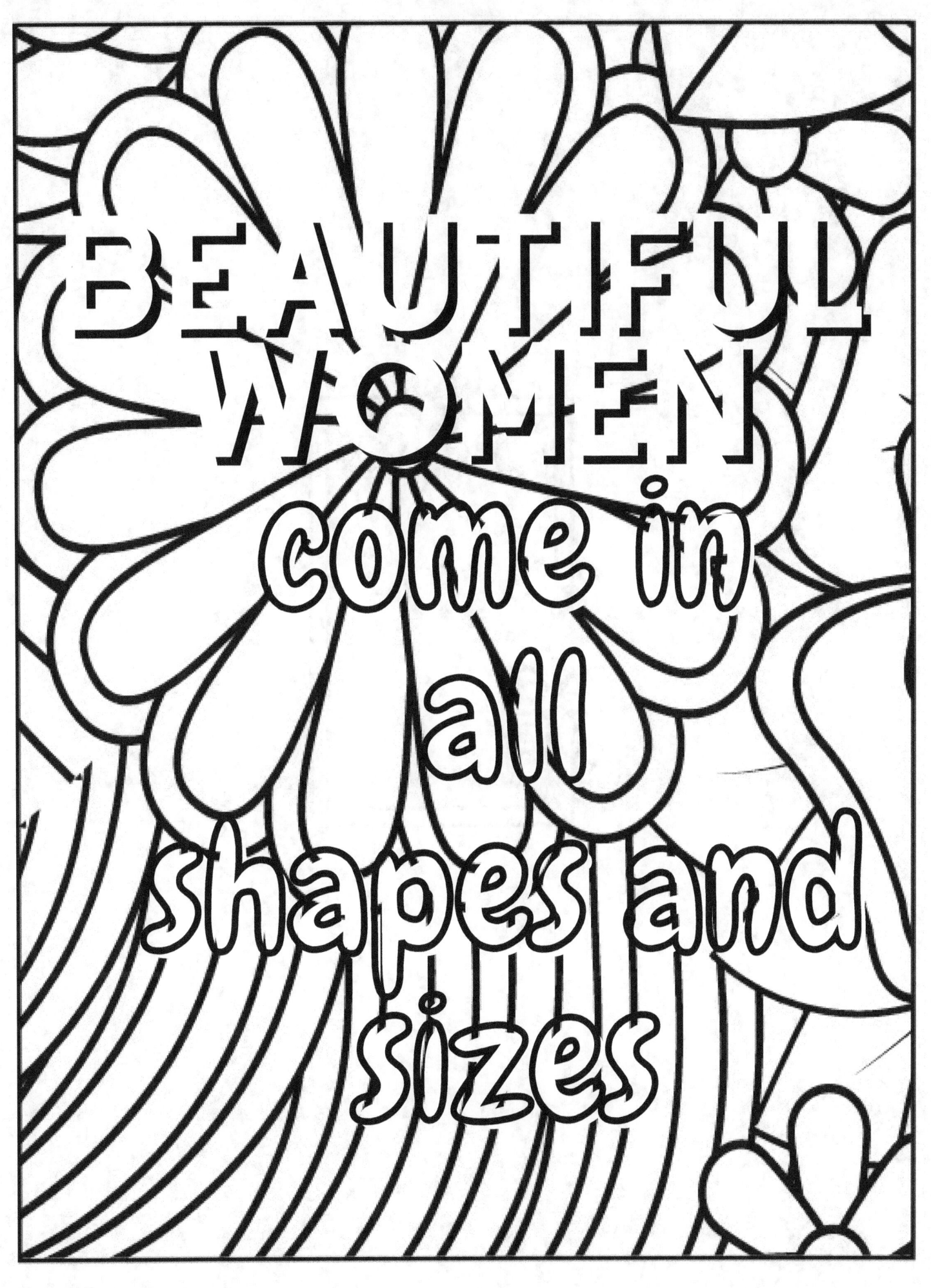

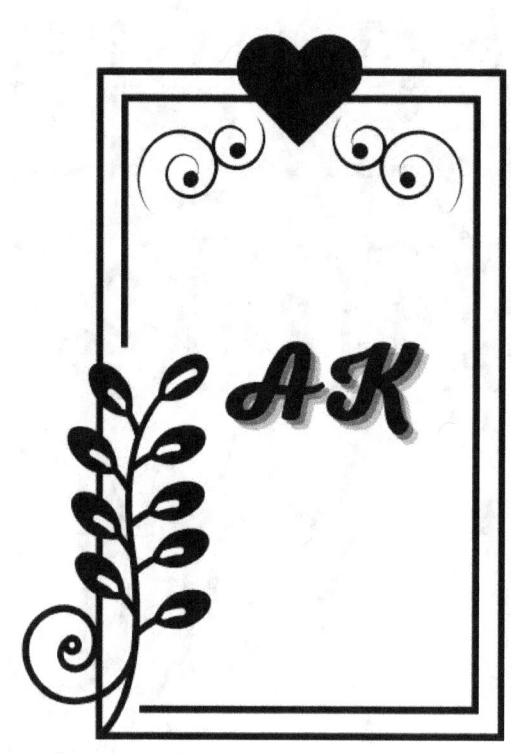

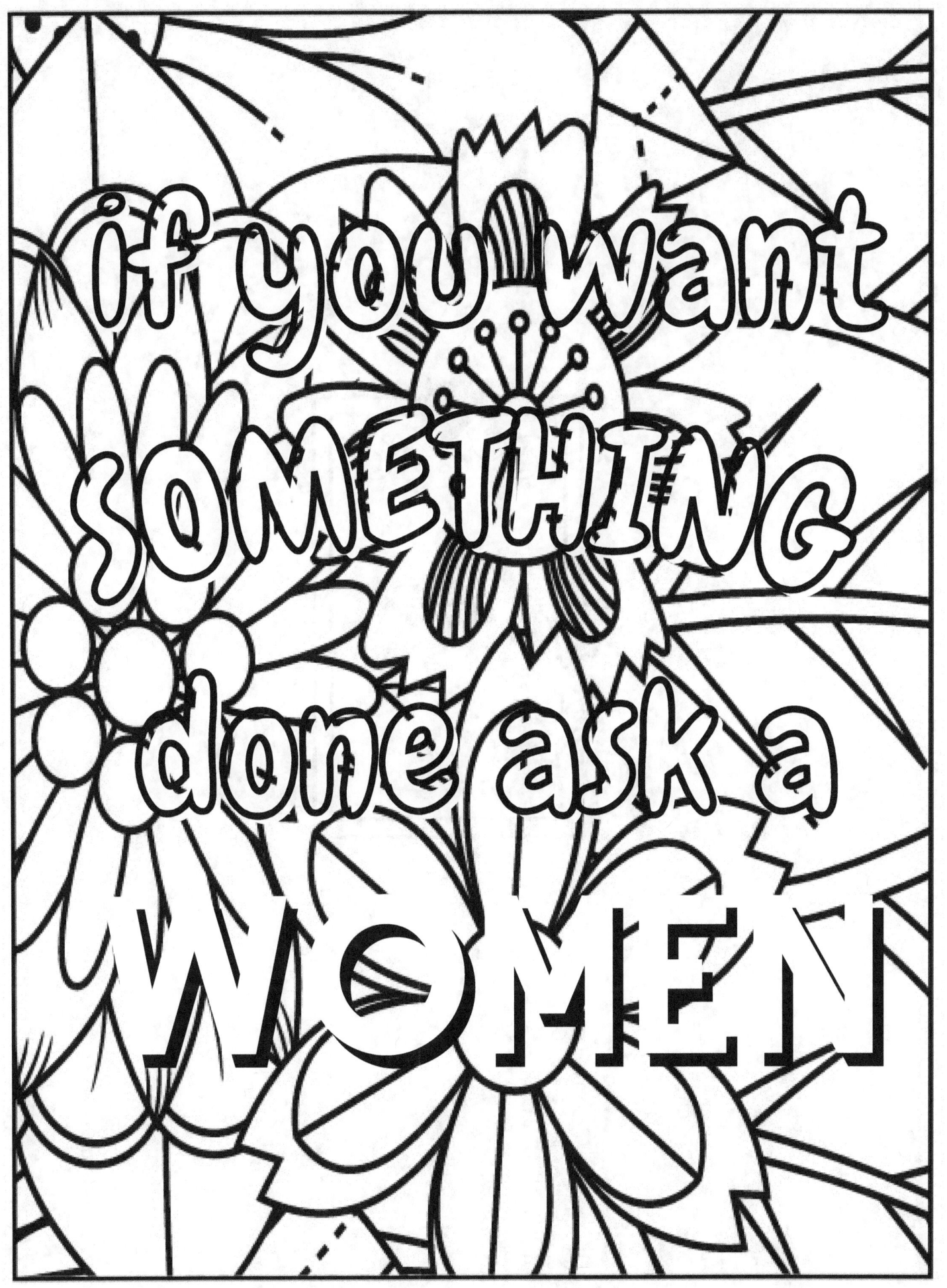

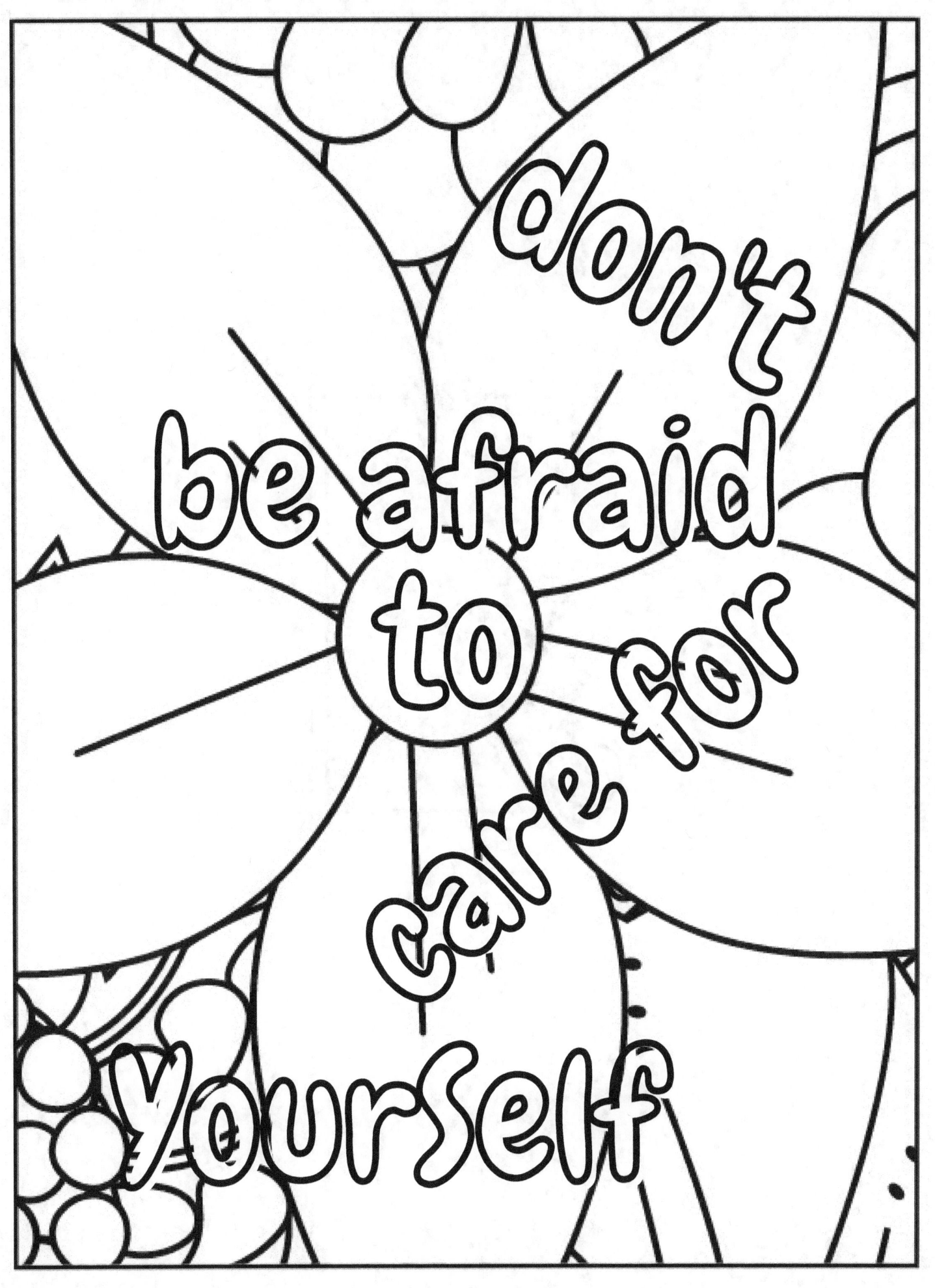

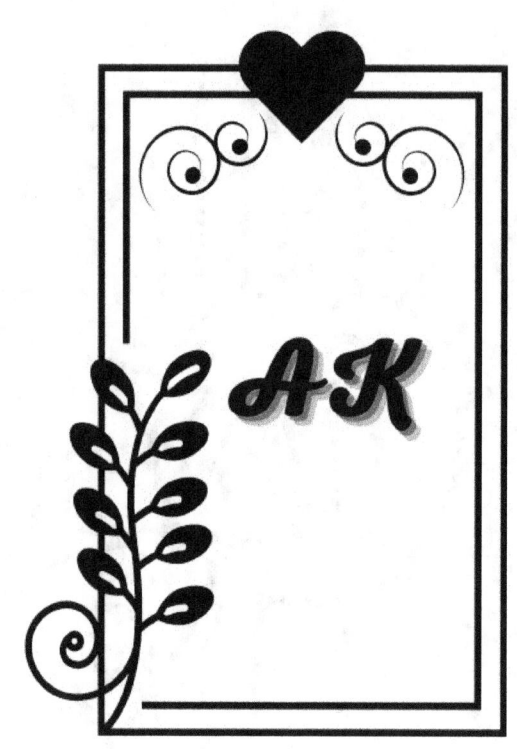

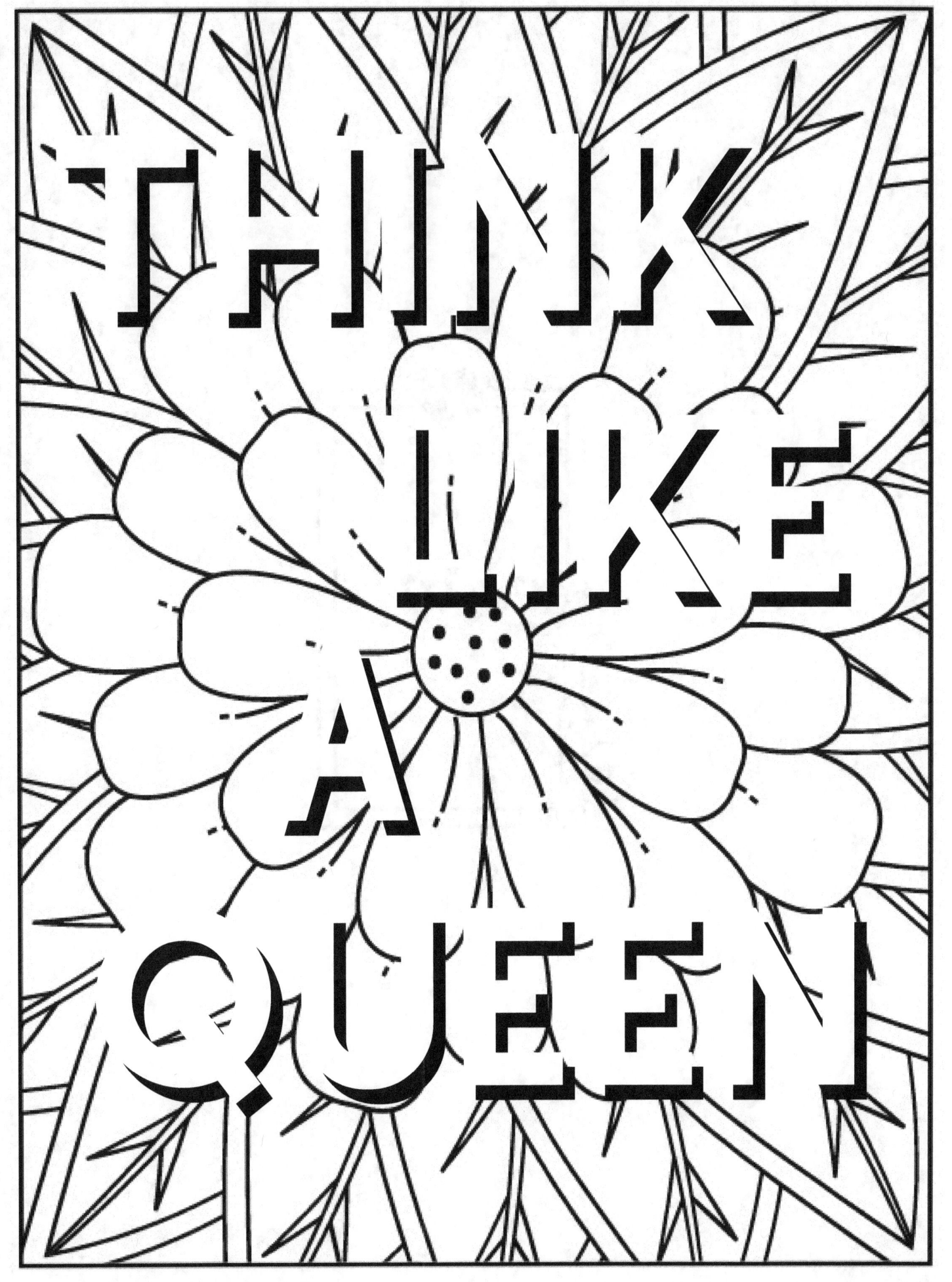

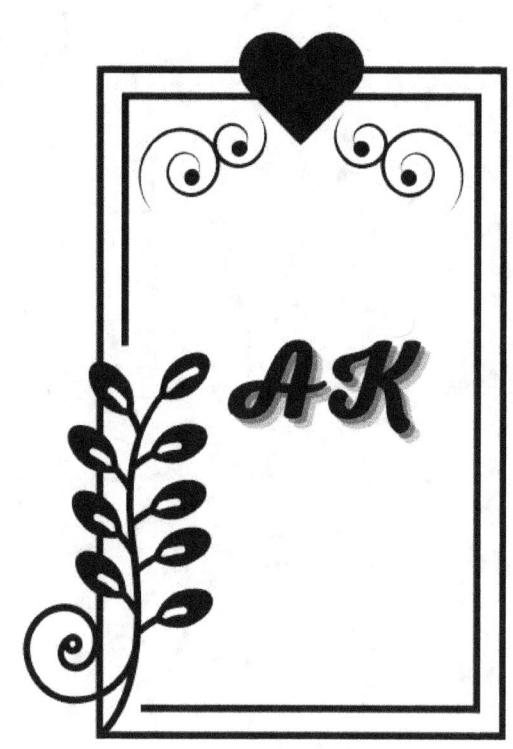

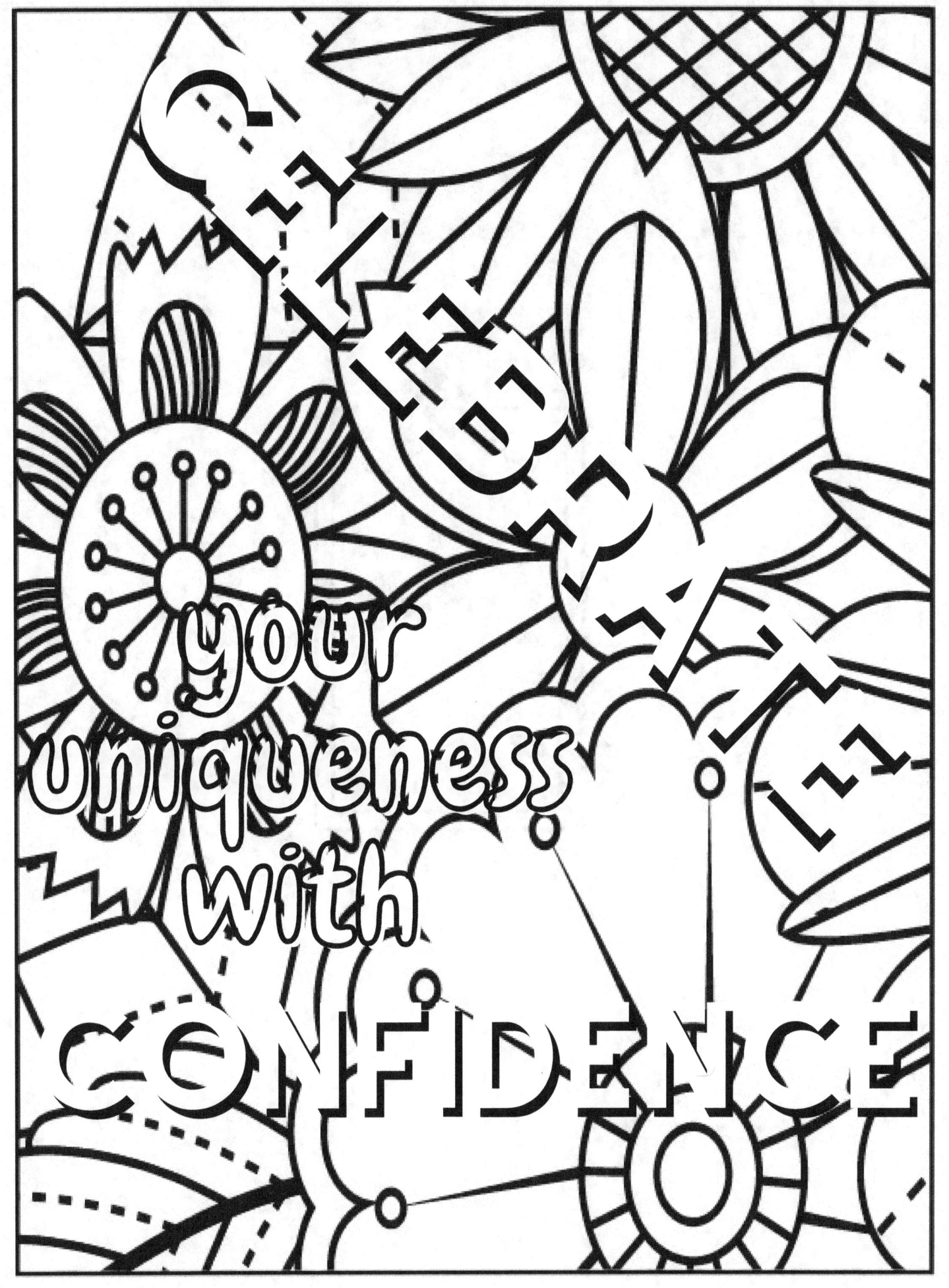

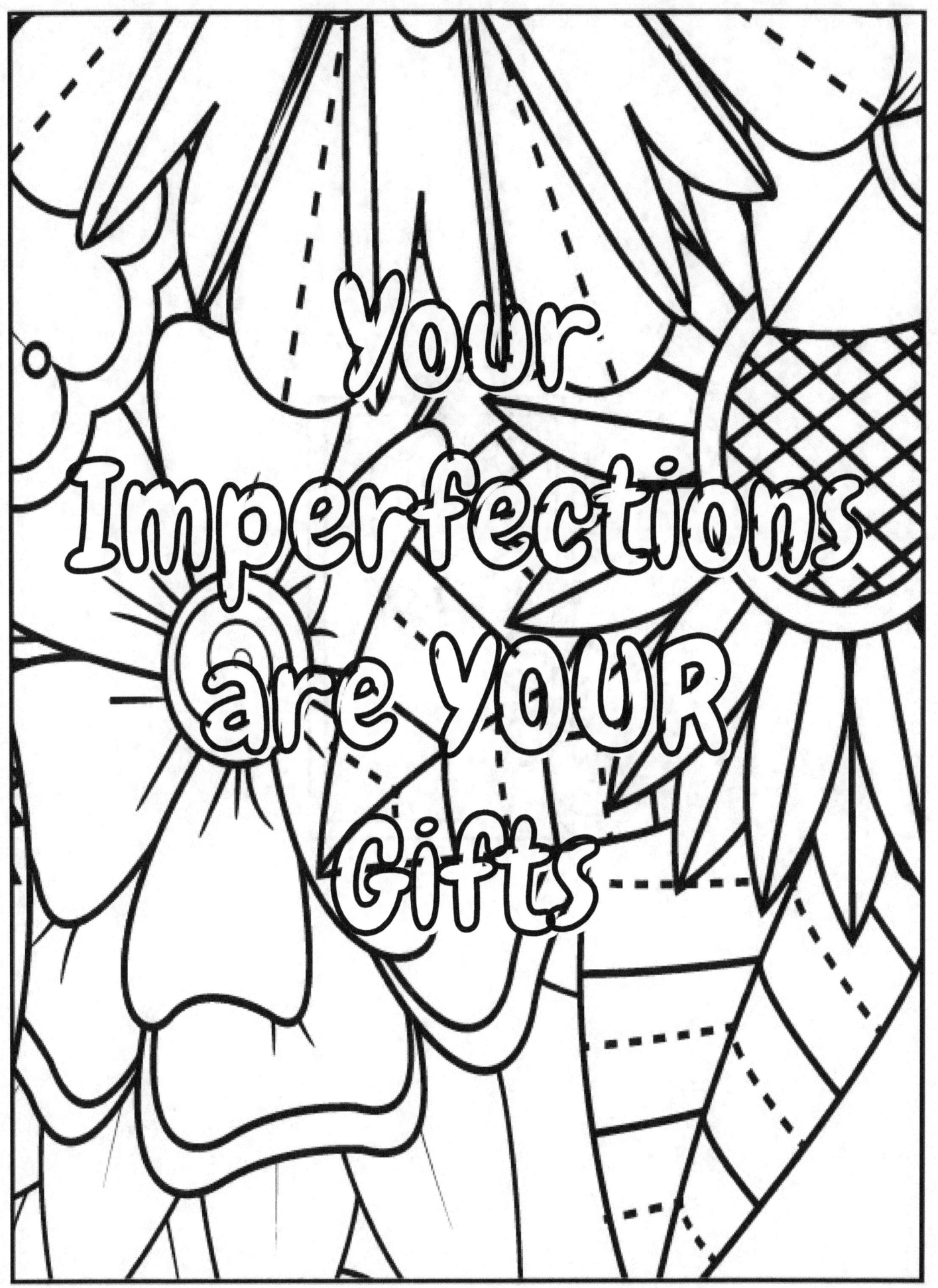

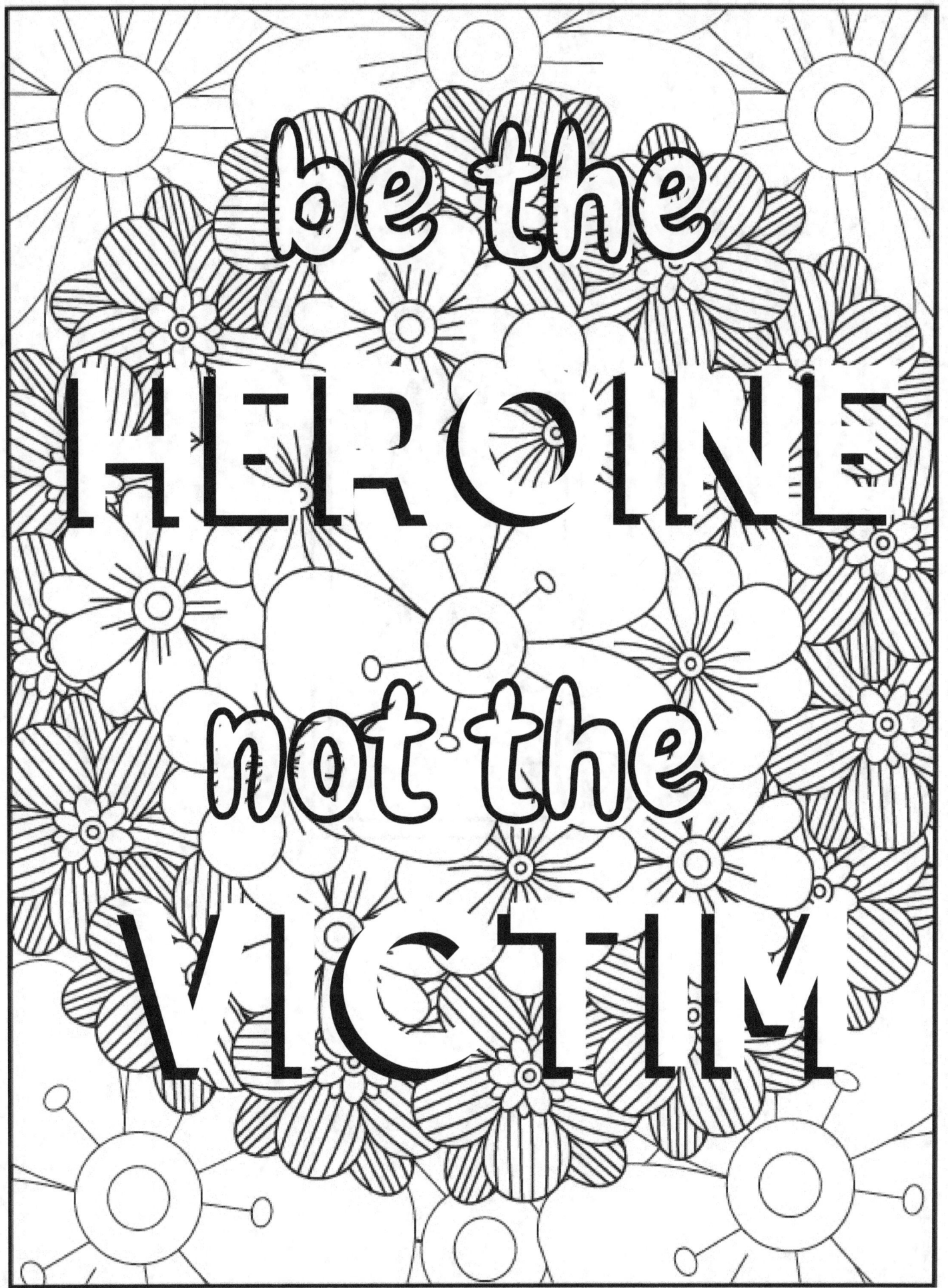

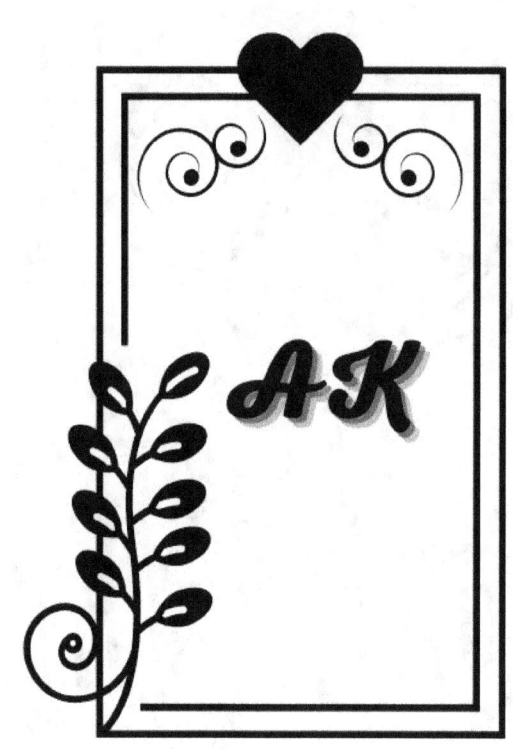

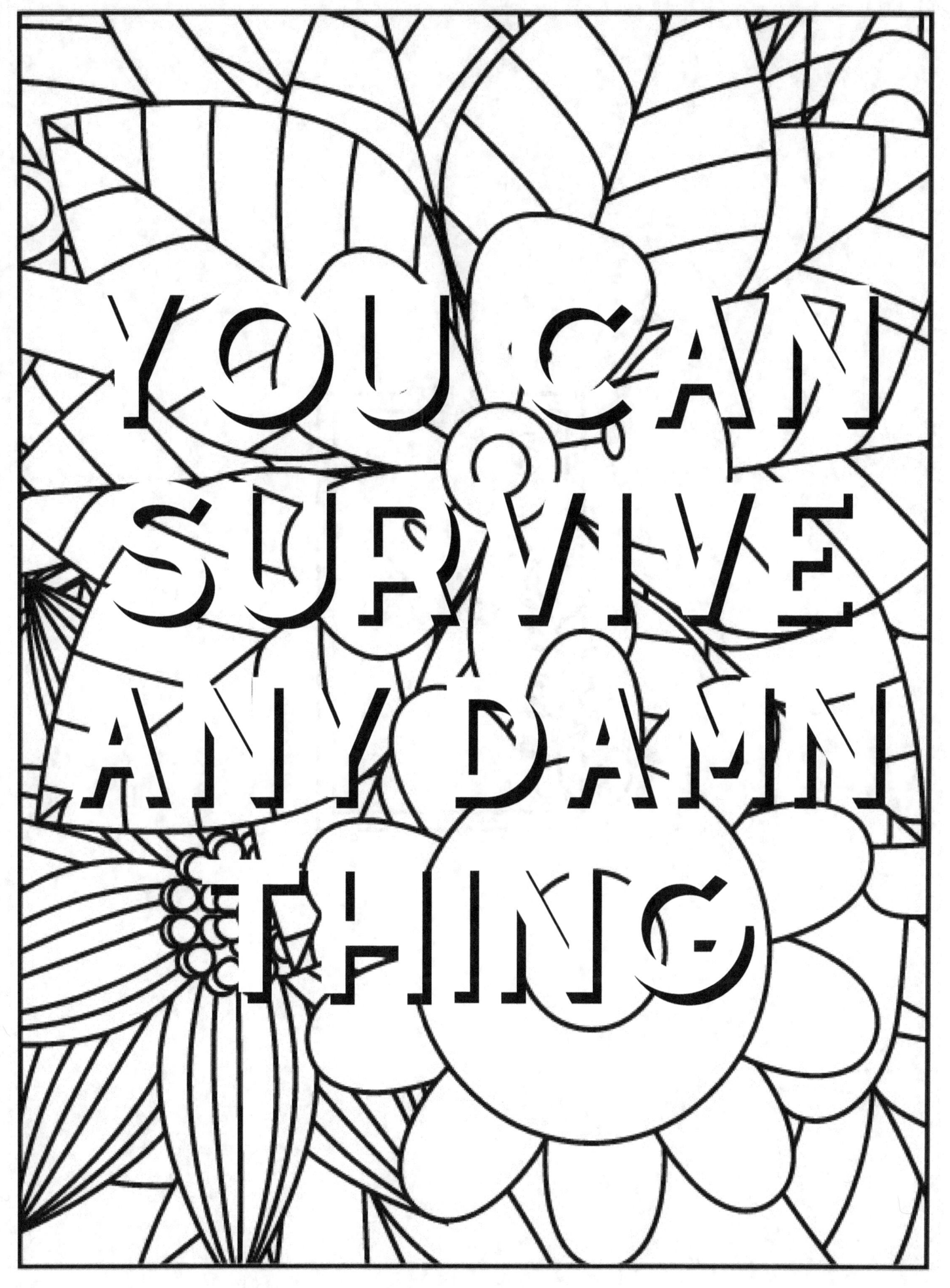

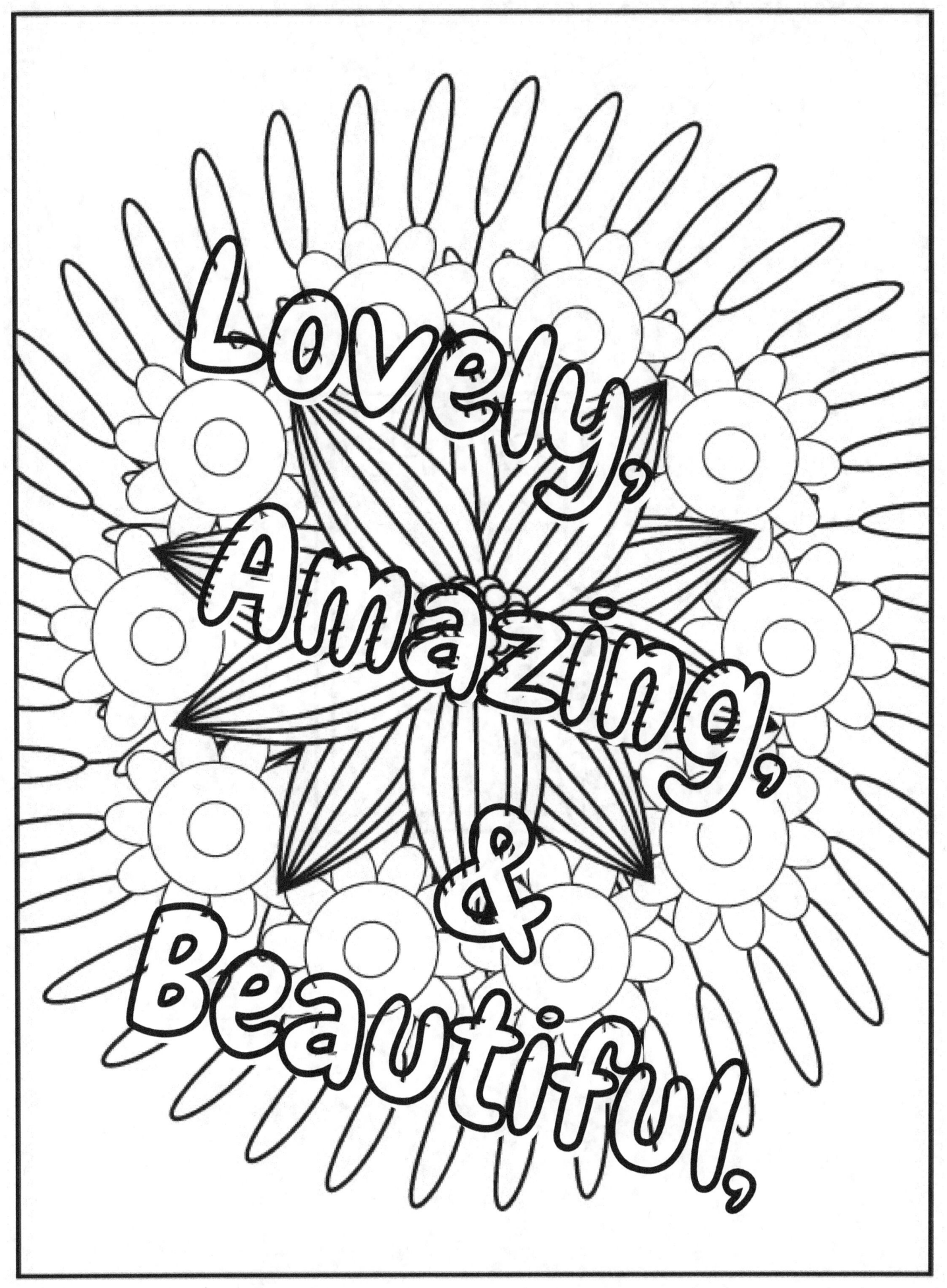

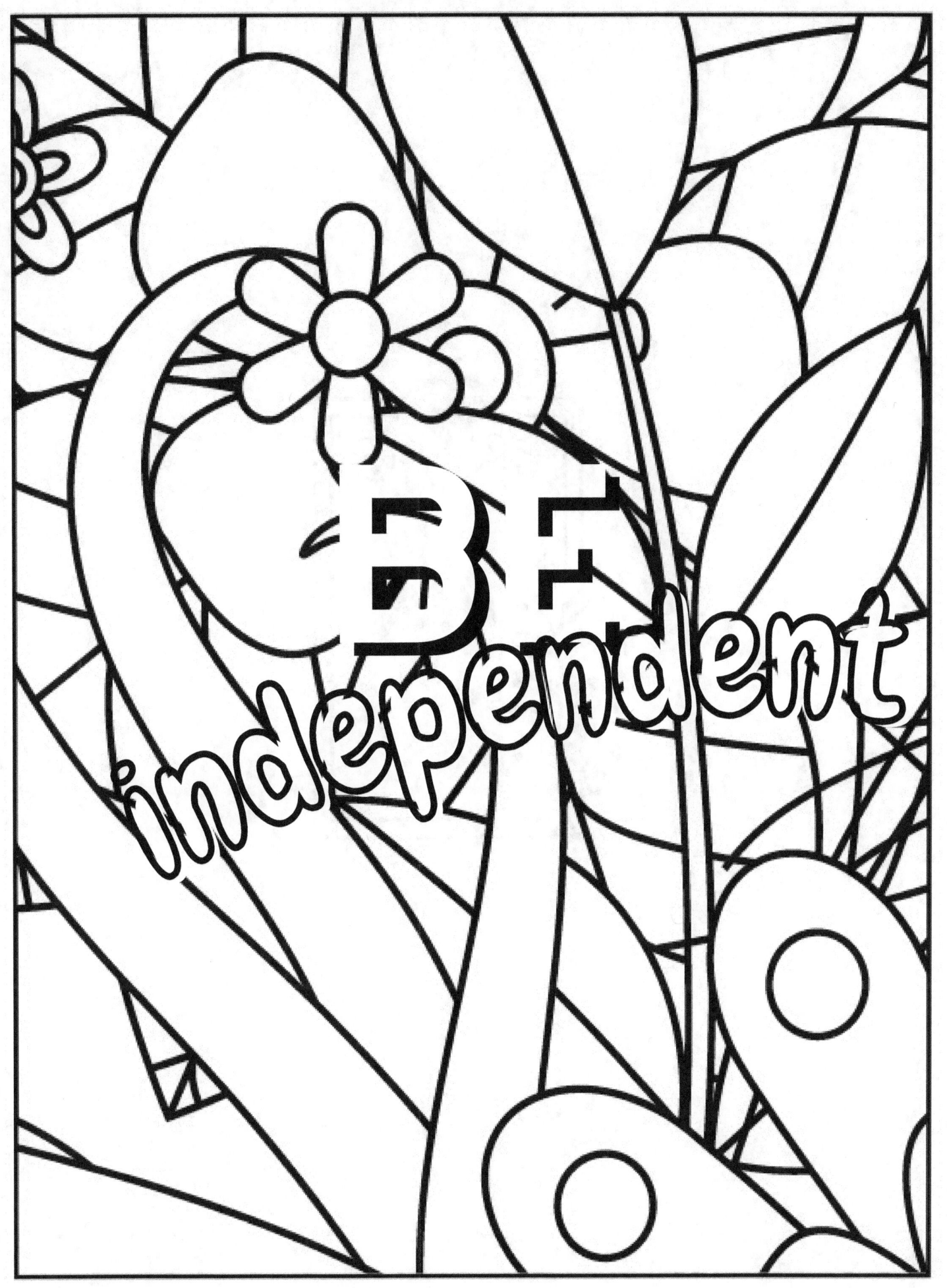

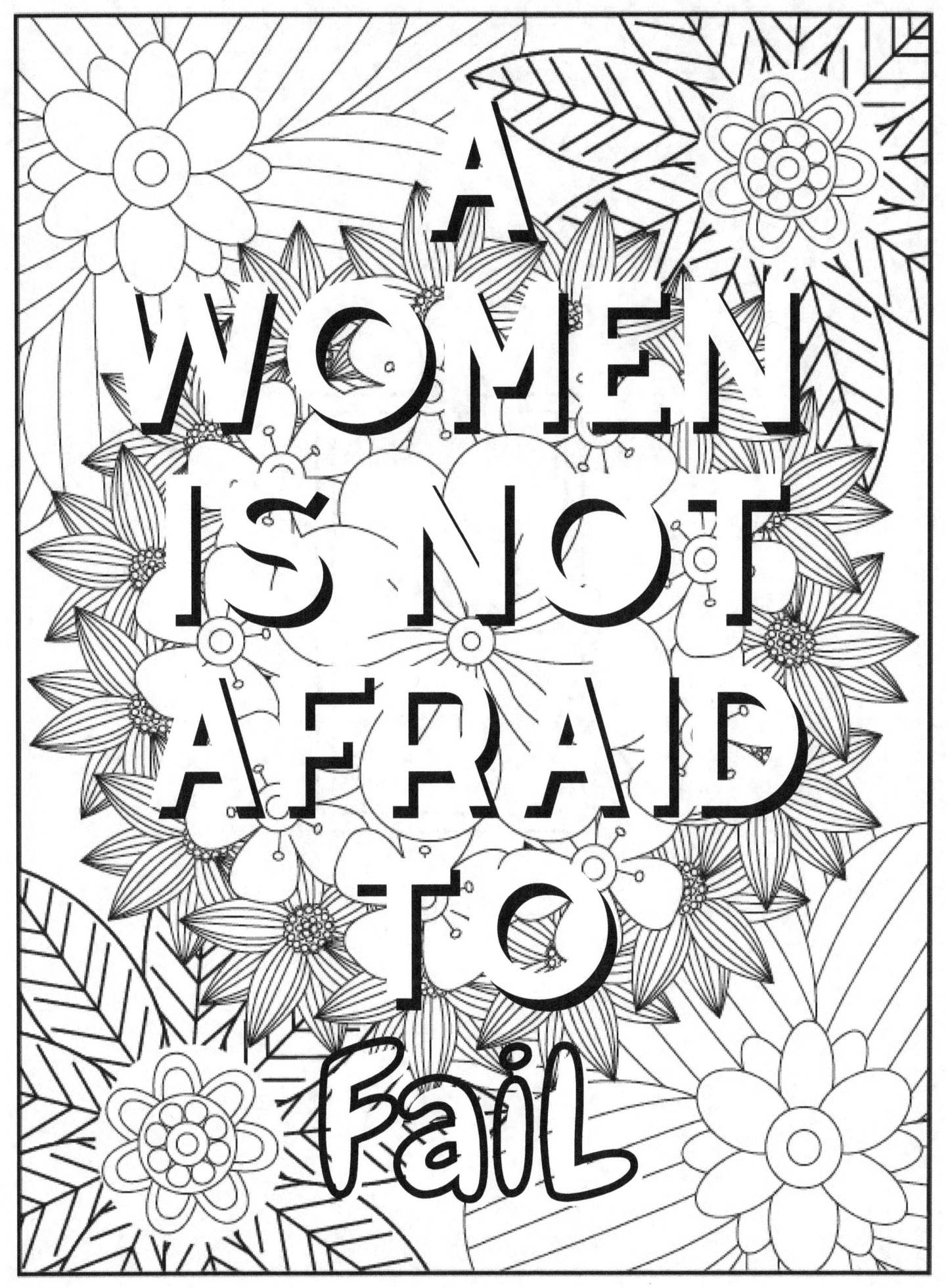

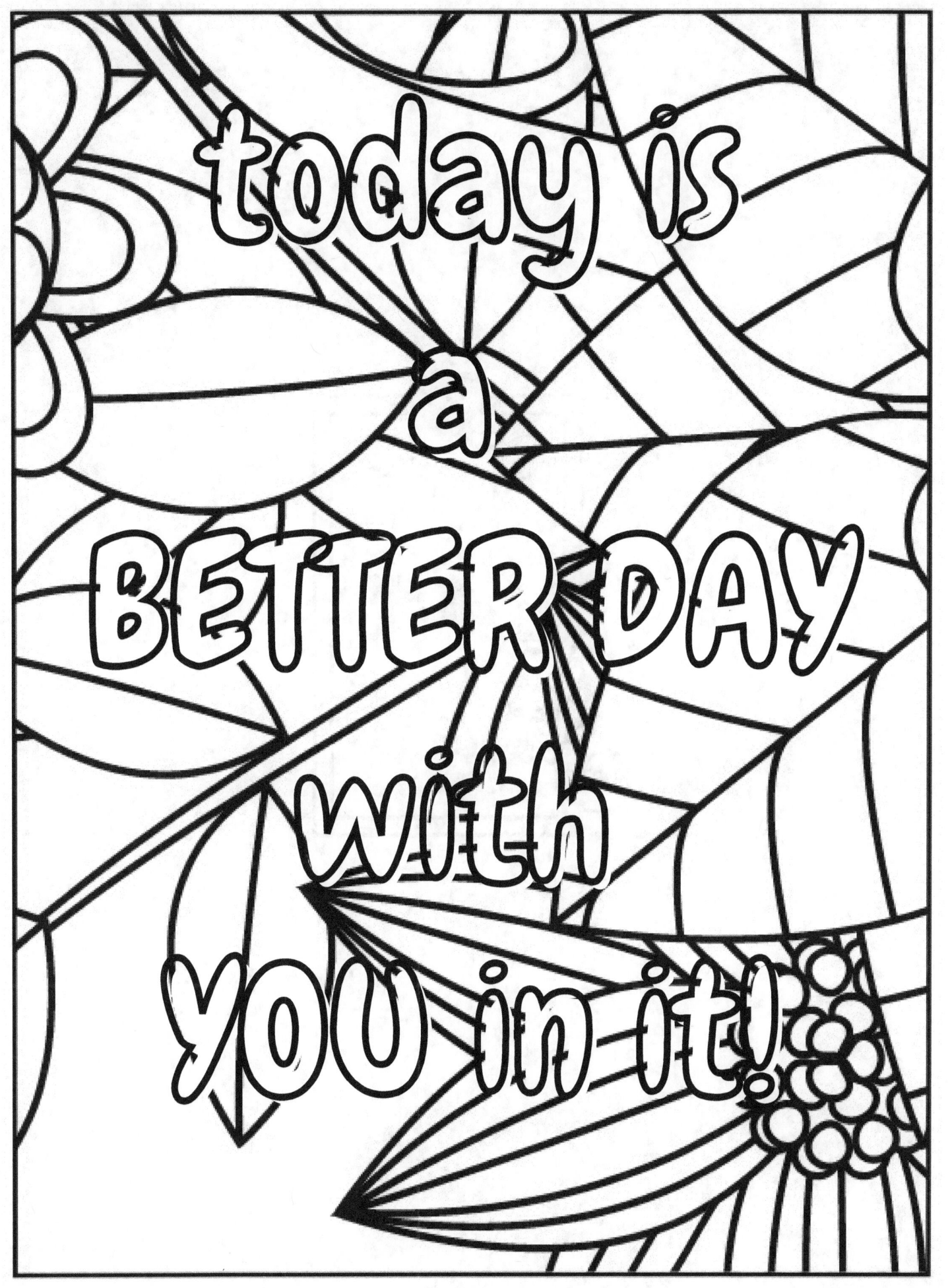

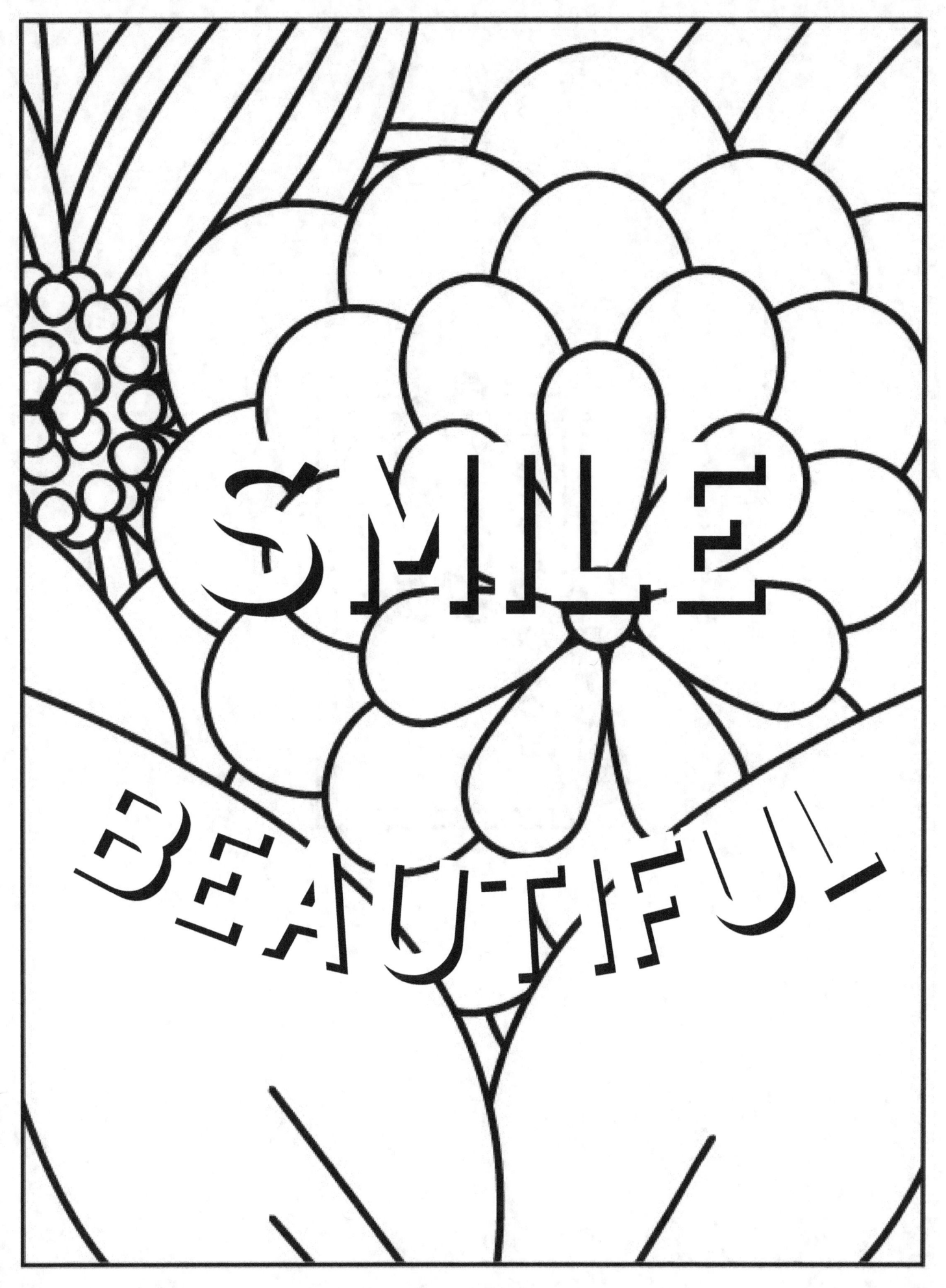

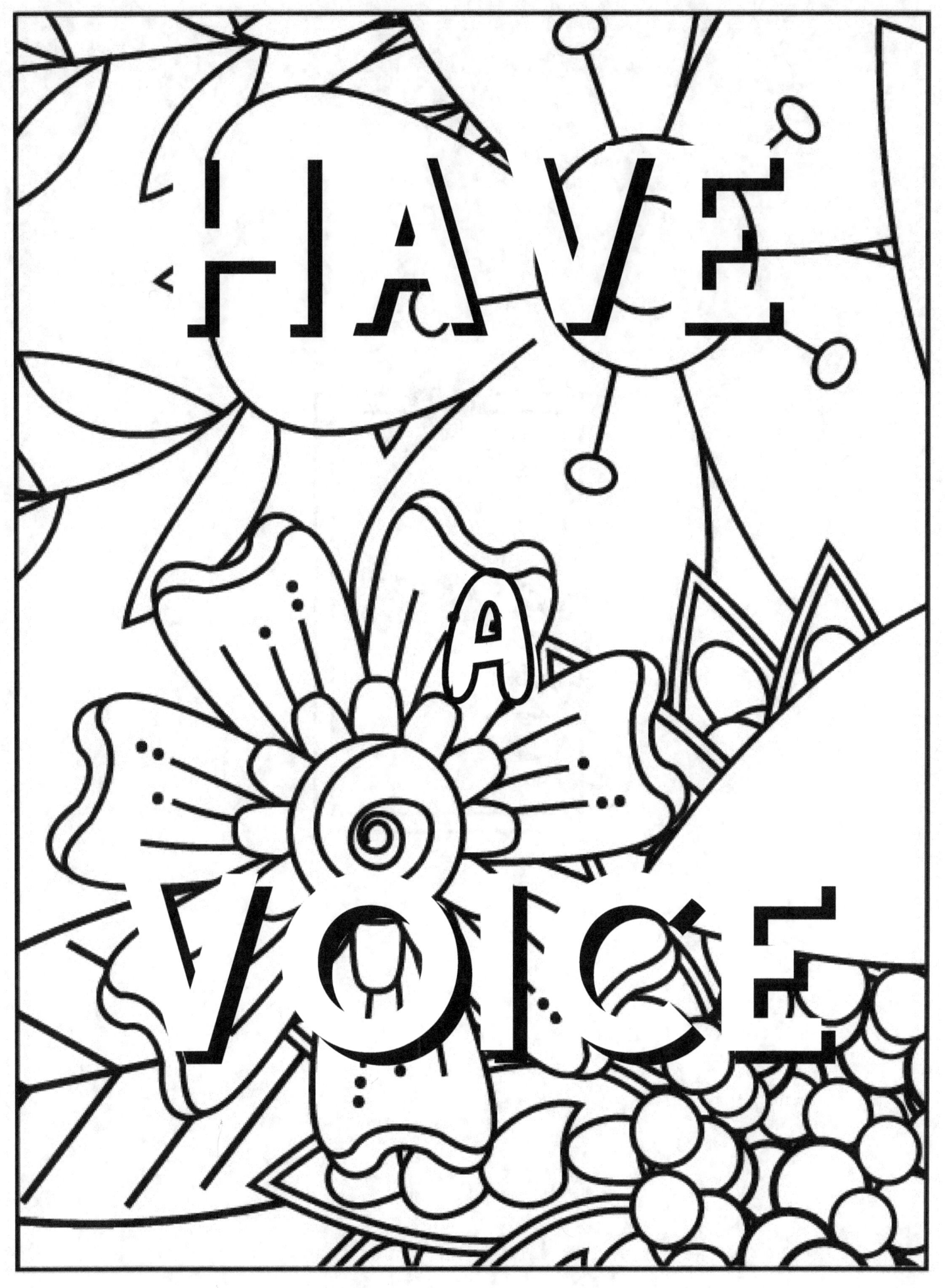

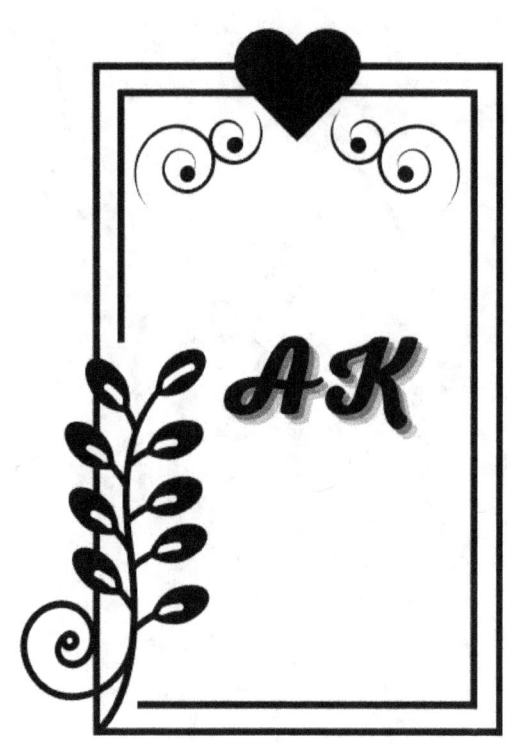

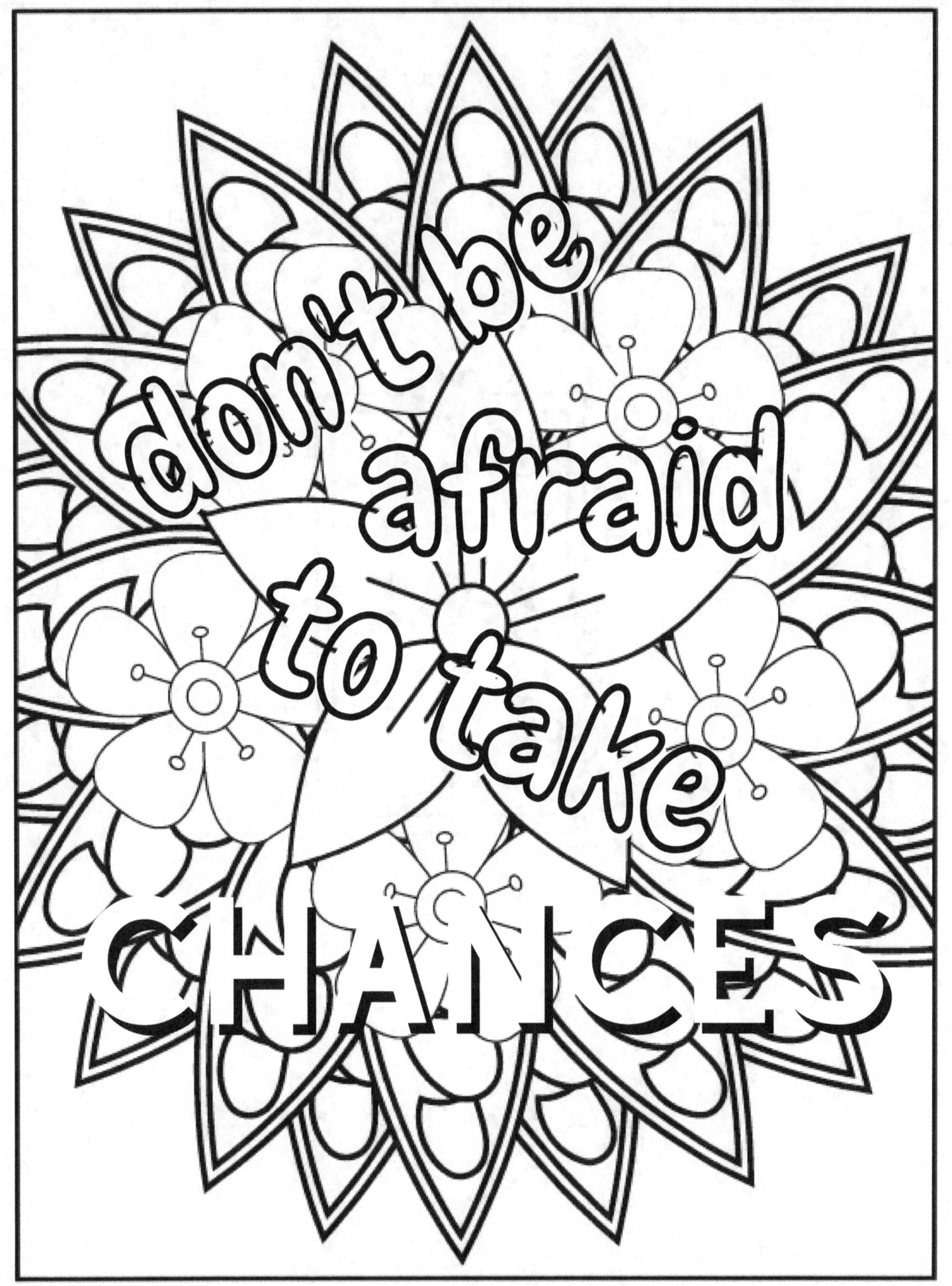

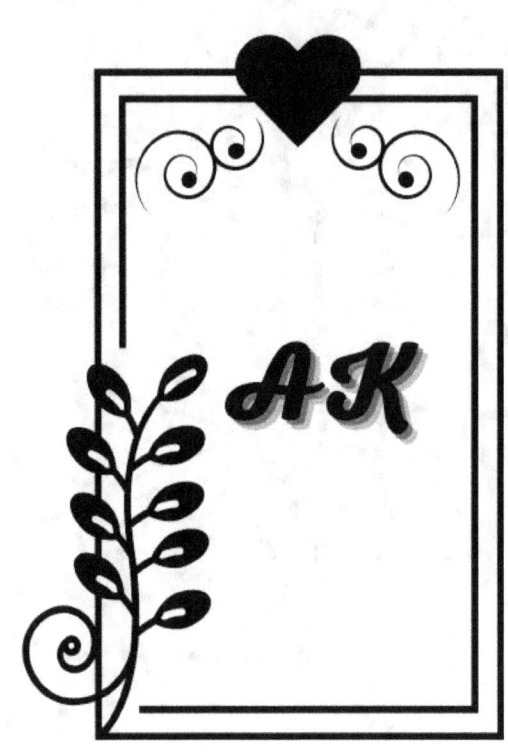

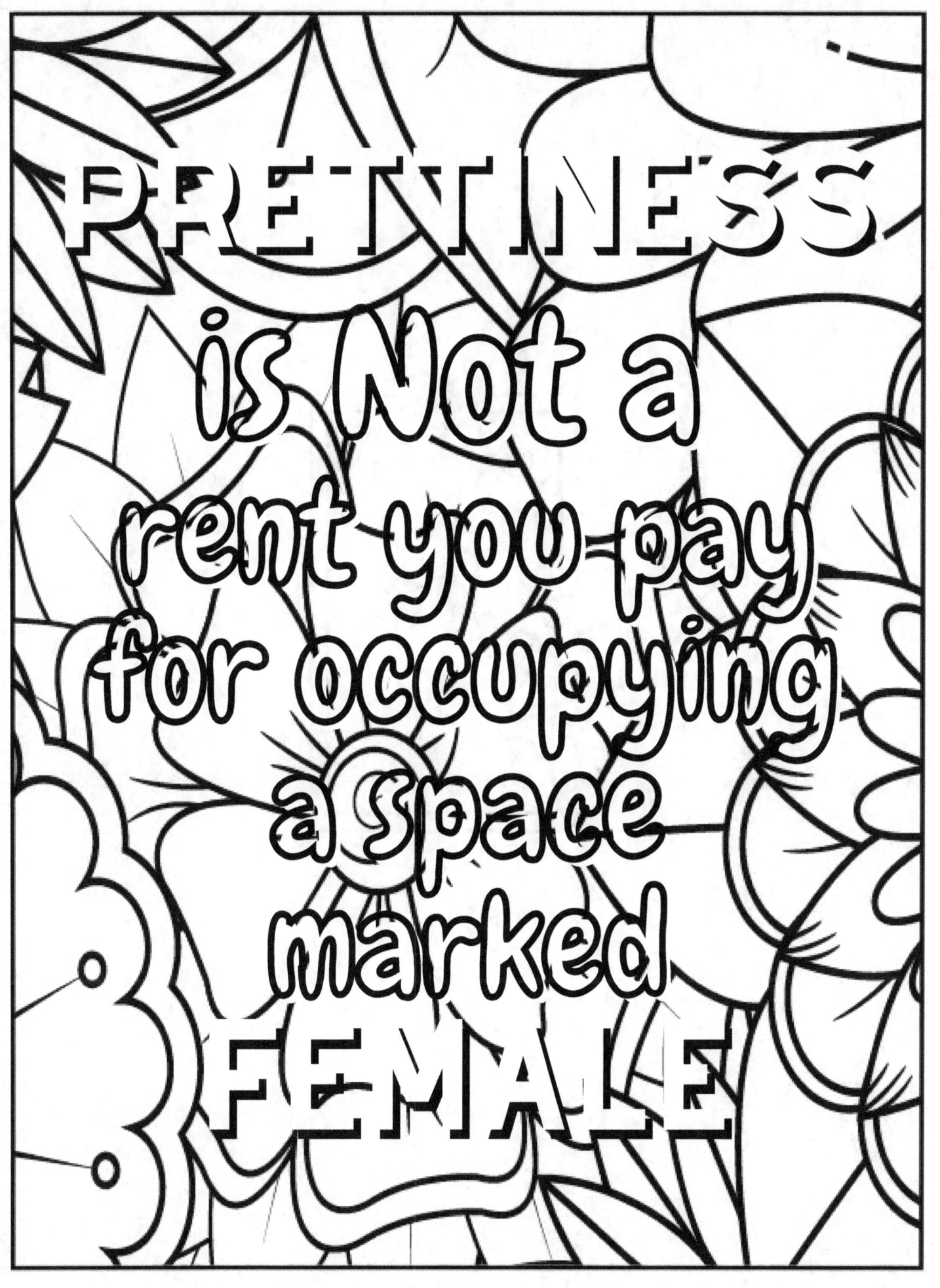

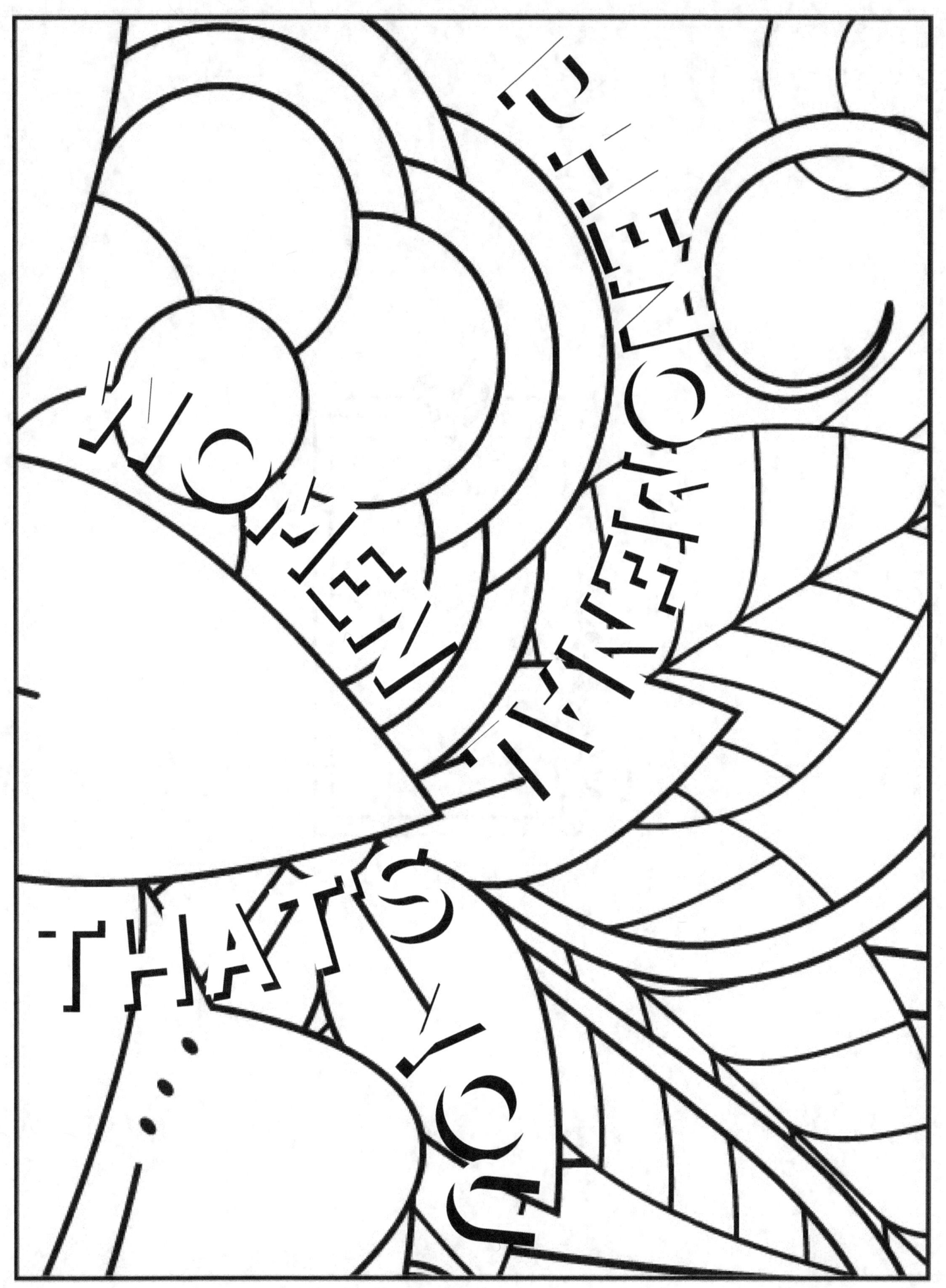

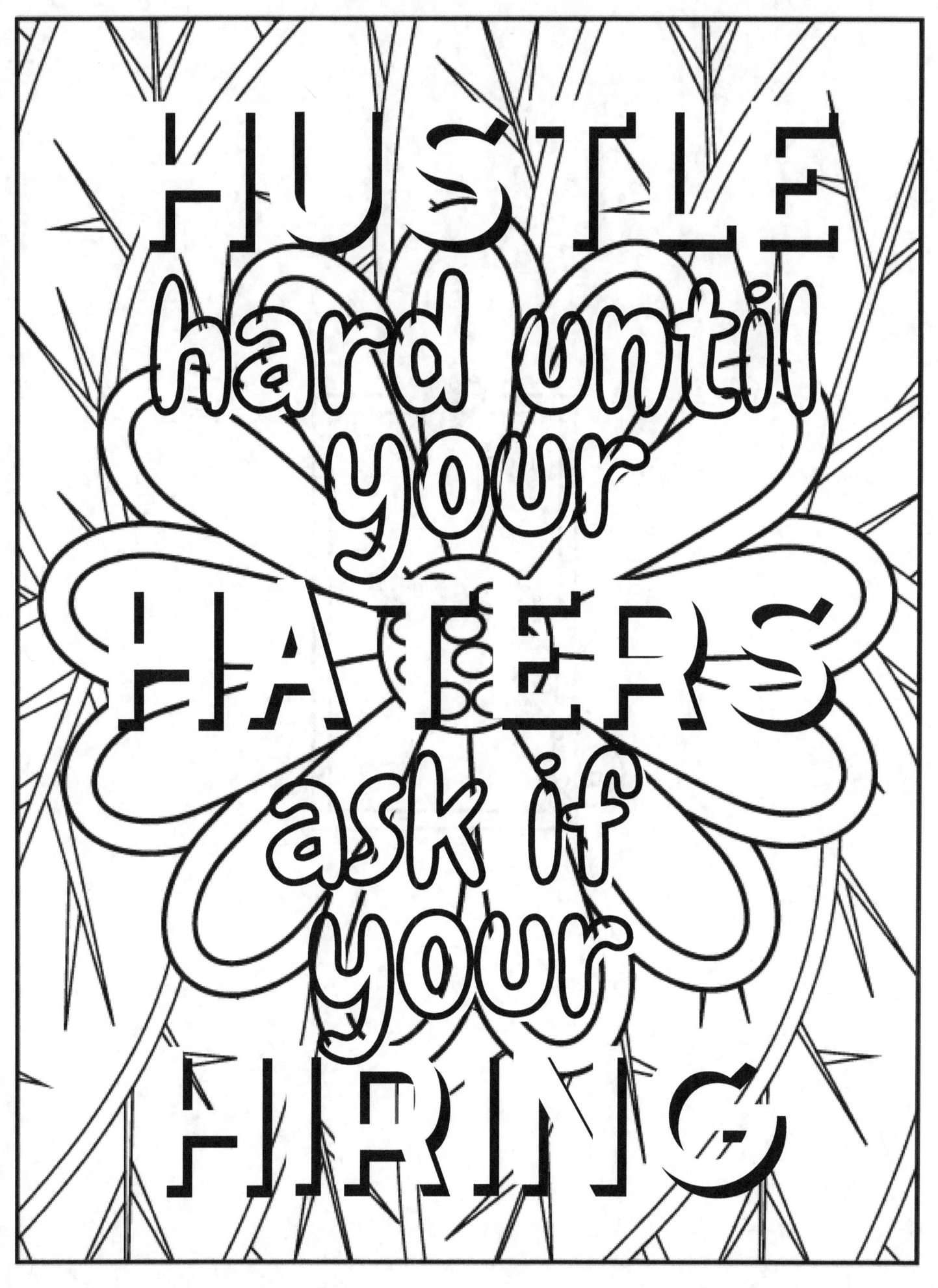

www.ingramcontent.com/pod-product-compliance
Lightning Source LLC
Chambersburg PA
CBHW082109220526
45472CB00009B/2105